Stronger

The Science and Art of Stress Resilience

Amit Sood MD MS FACP

ISBN 13: 978-0-9995525-1-3
ISBN 10: 0-9995525-1-1
Library of Congress Control Number: **2018914697**
LCCN Imprint Name: **Global Center for Resiliency and Wellbeing,
Rochester, MN**

Disclaimer

The information in this book is not intended to substitute a physician's advice or
medical care. Please consult your physician or other health care provider if you are
experiencing any symptoms or have questions pertaining to the information contained
in this book.

Resilience is the core strength you use to lift the load of life.

Resilience is doing well when you shouldn't be doing well.

Just as you can learn math, music, and language, you can learn resilience.

Resilience skills upgrade and strengthen your neuronal networks by leveraging your brain's ability to change itself with experience.

The result: Enhanced resilience lifts every aspect of your life— physical, emotional, social, occupational, and spiritual.

You have a choice in how you experience each passing moment. Choose the resilient option to live your day and your life to the fullest.

Contents

Less than perfect, but better than expected   2

Introduction   4

What is Resilience?

1. Resilience is a Story   11
2. Let's Define it Anyway   13
3. Resilience Research   16
4. Resilience versus Stress Management   20
5. Three Examples from Nature   23
6. How Vulnerability Can Make Us Resilient   25
7. The Four Domains   28
8. Resiliency Genes   36
9. The Brain Chemistry   40
10. Resilient Mindset   43
11. How Are You Resilient?   47

Why be Resilient?

12. Four Reasons   52
13. Resilience and Physical Health (Part 1)   57
14. Resilience and Physical Health (Part 2)   61
15. Resilience and Psychological Wellbeing   65
16. Resilience and Work   69
17. Resilience and Relationships   72
18. Summary   75

References   81

Acknowledgements   100

About Dr. Sood   101

To all the resilience researchers and teachers—past, present, and future.

Less than Perfect, But Better than Expected

It had been snowing for several days with the high of -5-degree Fahrenheit (minus the wind chill). The roads were a sheet of black ice, particularly the service and side roads. By 7:30 A.M., several cars had their noses buried in the snow, their tail lights blinking. Somehow, I made into the parking lot and tip toed inside the building. In the elevator were familiar faces, of colleagues rushing from one meeting to the next. Many had their eyes buried in smartphones—reviewing notes, answering emails, or feasting on the political theatre that now plays out every day and is available for mass consumption.

Thinking about the busy hours ahead, as I pressed the button for the twelfth floor, a familiar voice greeted me from behind.

"Hi, Dr. Sood, how are you doing this morning?" said Cindy, one of my colleagues from admin. Cindy is someone with whom I often share 20-second inspiring hallway conversations.

After a pause, I heard myself say, "Less than perfect, but better than expected!"

"That's so true, isn't it, particularly the way it looks outside today?" Cindy said. We shared a cordial laughter.

As I walked toward my office my words again rang in my head: *Less than perfect, but better than expected!* How true of a statement that is. I could have veered off the road. My car's battery could have died. I could have slipped on the pavement. But none of that happened.

I traveled back further. I woke up in a warm bed this morning, free of excruciating pain. I wasn't with anyone who yelled at me and made me feel unworthy. I had hot cereal for breakfast. The water didn't run out in the middle of my shower. My life was going pretty good (especially because all of these have happened at one point or another in my life).

My kids woke up without nose bleeds. My wife and I were able to negotiate all the morning tantrums. All the homeworks were complete and tucked away safely in the bags. Despite the rough drive, we didn't get a tardy ticket.

I zoomed out further. How lucky I am to be trusted by people who come from all around to see me. How lucky I am to be of service. I could have been born with a major congenital defect, in a toxic neighborhood, maybe even in a war-torn country. I could have acquired any number of serious infections that might have impaired my physical and cognitive abilities.

But none of that happened. And I am grateful.

Let it snow, let it be sub-zero. It's okay if I am overworked. It's okay if I don't have much of 'me time.' It's okay. As long as I am breathing and can serve a purpose dear to me, there's so much more right than there is wrong.

It was never meant to be perfect. And it is definitely better than expected. I am enough. I have enough.

Every day, I need to remind myself these six words (my personal golden rule): *I am enough. I have enough.* They provide me with immediate comfort. They pull me away from the left lane. They help me face adversity with fortitude. I stop dwelling on the thought of 'poor me.' I become a little stronger, a little more resilient.

This book is a day-long trolley ride into the science and perspectives that will help you understand resilience, and perhaps inspire you to embrace the resilient option. This isn't a 'how to resilience' type guide. It is more a survey of understanding the concepts of resilience and why you might care about it. It melds both art and science, with a slight edge toward science.

Somewhere along this journey, try and examine your life. Perhaps you might have the same thought about your life as I had that snowy day—Less than perfect, but better than expected.

Thank you for trusting me with your time.

Amit

Introduction

Hundreds of islands spread out over 1500 miles come together to create the 50th state of the United States—Hawaii. Hawaii's warm tropical climate, public beaches, and picturesque landscape invite over eight million tourists each year. But it hasn't always been that way. Over the last two-hundred years, Hawaiian people have had to adapt to dizzyingly large shifts in political, military, and business interests. Several industries have come and gone, some in a span of just a few decades.

Sandalwood emerged in the 1810s, but faded in the 1830s, to be replaced by whaling. Whaling passed the baton to sugarcane in the 1870s. After several decades of a good run, sugar went sour in the mid 1950s, because of growing competition, increasing cost of labor, and international politics. However, two big changes that both happened in 1959 came to the rescue—one, Hawaii achieved statehood, and two, commercial jet service started in the U.S. Simultaneously, a booming economy spawned a cohort of stressed-out people with dispensable incomes who loved to quiet their nerves with the deep breaths of paradise. Soon, the acres and acres of plantations got converted into hotels and resorts, transforming tiny Hawaii into one of the top ten visited states in the U.S.A.

Hawaii is an excellent example of resilience by both its ability to adapt to dramatic changes, many not in its control, and its capacity to bounce back from a series of setbacks. Hawaii now boasts an unemployment rate of near three percent, better than California, Colorado, and Massachusetts. No wonder our journey into resilience starts in this resilient land—in Kauai, the fourth largest Hawaiian island.

Kauai Longitudinal Study

Psychologist Emmy E Werner from UC Davis and Ruth Smith, a Kauai psychologist set up a very interesting study in 1955.[1] Until then most studies on mental health focused on risk factors and went back in time (retrospective). Werner-Smith designed a study to look into the future (prospective). While this may seem simple and obvious now, it was phenomenally innovative in its time.

Werner-Smith put together a team of committed pediatricians, public health nurses, mental health workers, and social workers and enrolled all Kauai newborns for the year 1955—698 of them. These babies were then followed at ages 1, 2, 10, 18, 32, and 40 to assess the impact of different risk and protective factors on their lives.[2]

As you can discern from the changing and struggling economy of Hawaii in the 1950s, a full one third of the 698 babies, 210 to be precise, were considered at high risk due to one or more of the following four factors—pre or perinatal complications, poverty, daily instability (chronic discord, divorce, serious parental mental health issues), and mothers with less than eight grades of education. On follow up, by age 10, two thirds of these children developed learning or behavior problems, and by age 18, had developed mental health issues and/or delinquency. To the team's surprise, 72 vulnerable children (about a third) were doing very well. They were caring, kind, and successful. They had a rewarding social life, no trouble with the law, and kept as good if not better jobs than their peers with much more privileged background. They were also healthier than their average peers. These children were *resilient*.

This was a remarkable finding because most studies prior to Werner and Smith's enrolled children who weren't doing well, emotionally or behaviorally. These studies went back to look for troubles in the past. Troubles like history of abuse, alcoholism, parental mental illness, family discord, and more. This retrospective look had painted a dark picture. 'Adverse life situations invariably portend bad outcomes,' was the prevailing mantra. Researchers had no idea that strength could emerge from weakness.

The Three Factors

When Werner and Smith dug deeper, they found three set of factors explaining resilience:

#1. Individual—Many children came programmed with a personality type that helped them adapt better. At age one, they were good natured, active and easy to deal with; at age two, cheerful, friendly, and sociable; at age 10, better readers, problem solvers, and helpers. As they grew older, they trusted their abilities, had better sense of control over their life, and were filled with hope. They were also very good at finding support.

#2. Family—Most of the resilient children had at least one emotionally stable caring person in their life. This person didn't have to be the parent. Sibling, uncle, aunt, grandparent—anyone would do. These children also commonly had a family tradition that offered them the construct of faith in a higher power, that provided them meaning.

#3. Community—Often, the resilient children were surrounded by a supportive larger community, particularly during times of crisis—teachers, neighbors, elders, friends' parents, church members, youth leaders, and many others.

As these children grew older, there was even more reason for hope. Most of the struggling youth had recovered when researchers met them at age 32 or 40. Having a secure meaning through work, relationship, and faith helped. Finding an emotionally stable partner and a stable job were two strong resilience factors. For some who became acutely sick or injured, recovery from a life-threatening condition provided the perspective to develop resilience.

Werner and Smith were not alone in this groundbreaking research. Around the same time, several other groups including Michael Rutter who studied children in inner city London and Isle of Wight and Norman Garmezy who followed children of mothers with schizophrenia in Minneapolis, Minnesota, reported similar findings and found roughly that the same three group of factors influence a positive outcome: individual personality, family ties and cohesion, and external support systems.[3] These core findings have now been replicated in multiple populations in over a dozen longitudinal studies including studies in Australia, New Zealand, Denmark, Sweden, Switzerland, UK, Germany, and USA.

Resilience (and Vulnerability) in Adults

The trajectory of research in adults, although not as deep, is similar. In adults, the older 18th and 19th-century science, particularly psychological science was focused on illness. The model is now thankfully shifting toward wellness. The statistics reveal: 75 percent of U.S. population doesn't have diagnosed emotional or behavioral problems;[4] Of the 50-60 percent who get exposed to significant traumatic events in their life time, most do not develop post-traumatic stress disorder (PTSD);[5,6] (8-20 percent of these develop PTSD).[7,8] After deployment, the most common outcome is low stress or resilience and not psychopathology (80 percent).[9]

But all is not well. Not being actively suicidal or not experiencing severe anxiety, although a good start, isn't the same as flourishing. By most measures, improvement in our psychological wellbeing and happiness has lagged behind growth in our gross domestic product. We are working very hard but not enjoying our success. Over 80 percent of workers experience excessive stress on the job.[10] A full 70 percent of us are not fully engaged at work.[11] Over 60 percent experience day to day discrimination such as receiving poor service, feeling threatened or harassed, or burdened with less than courteous treatment.[12] More than 65 percent health care professionals today are experiencing burnout—a state of fatigue, cynicism, and/or a sense of low personal accomplishment.[13] Depression is the leading cause of disability globally, affecting over 300 million people.[14] These are very high numbers.

I see every day, in my medical practice and life, the kindest, most wonderful people, struggling for no fault of theirs. The national trends are disturbing. Despite all our efforts to stem the tide of self-harm, the numbers continue to inch upward. Our current suicide rate is the highest it has been in three decades, with approximately 47,000 people taking their lives every year in the U.S. alone.[15] That is 129 citizens every day. Clearly more needs to be done to help support those who are struggling.

The Two Solutions

Excessive load can be tackled in two different ways. The first option is to decrease the load. This can be done by balancing demand with resources, providing more control, decreasing responsibilities, improving efficiency, providing better health care, social services, and more. This is essential but can only go so far because of two reasons:

1. The world is accelerating faster than our individual ability to adapt. This is because our society incentivizes speed. Whatever we incentivize, that's the direction we grow. The brain, however, has its limits, clearly exceeded now by the cognitive and emotional load of today—the proximate cause of widespread unrest.

2. Decreasing the load has its own costs. Offering 20 percent free time to the workers isn't practical when we have high capital demands and/or have to beat the average analyst estimates so our stock can maintain its valuation. You wouldn't ever hear a leader saying let's do less for more.

So, while lowering the load is an essential part of the equation, it alone won't suffice. Hence the need for a second solution, which is to increase our ability to lift the load—the resilient option. This book offers research supporting the resilient option. I believe resilience is an under-utilized solution that is now ready for prime time.

The Three Questions

As a researcher, physician and caring citizen, I strive every day to help people live a happier and more fulfilling life. In my effort to conceptualize and create a well-paved path to resilience, a worthy albeit ambitious undertaking, here are the three critical questions that I ask –

#1. Why do some people continue to thrive despite facing adversity?

#2. Can we replicate ideas and mindset of the resilient people to help everyone, particularly those who are struggling?

#3. Can we test some of these approaches in a structured and practical program and then offer that program in an easy to learn, engaging, and fun format?

Here is the good news: all this work has already been done!

I have covered the second and third questions in my previous books[16] and will expand on this topic more in another manuscript that will follow this one.

Through this book I will walk alongside you to share the essence of resilience research across a variety of disciplines with an aim to answer the first question.

The six words that can help you get insight into any problem are—when, where, who, what, why, and how. For resilience, the first three have obvious answers—when: we need greater resilience now; where: on our planet; who: for all of us. This book will answer the next two questions—what and why.

Before we launch, I want to share one additional perspective: keep in mind that resilience can only go so far. If you are constantly sleep deprived, nagged, financially constrained or in pain, it will be difficult for resilience to overcome all this in the short run. Resilience might help numb the pain a little and help you feel centered so you can make more rational decisions, but do not be disappointed in yourself if your equilibrium is disturbed in such situations. Resilience doesn't mean total invulnerability. Resilience also doesn't mean being unreal. It means, as we shall soon see, greater strength amidst vulnerability. So be kind with someone who is struggling, including yourself.

I

What is Resilience?

1. Resilience is a Story

The word resilience has trekked in my brain's networks for over two decades now. I have met experts, watched videos, read books and journal articles, developed and taught a structured resilience program, conducted and published research studies, played with words and concepts, written books, and most importantly, thought a lot. Recently I had an important realization. During most of my talks on resilience, when I provide definitions—short or long, catchy or cluttered, I find people yawning. But the moment I start sharing stories, they lean forward, eyes brighten, brains get engaged, eager to absorb inspiring details about what it means to survive as a human in this crazy scary world.

Hence my conclusion—resilience is more about stories, less about definitions. The fabric of our world is woven with the thread of stories. Stories help us overcome the limits of language in authentic expressions of feelings and inspirations.

We create stories and the stories then create us. Philosophically, all that will be left of you and me, at the end of our life, will be a story, hopefully a good one. Let me start by sharing with you a cute little resilience story—about a starfish.

Sallie the Starfish

About two years ago, I went to pick up our five-year-old daughter, Sia, from day care. She showed me a clay figure she had worked on all afternoon. It was a purple starfish, named Sallie. Purple was her favorite color at that time. She was bubbling with energy, really excited to show her production to my then eleven-year-old daughter, Gauri, my wife, and me.

Unfortunately, as we got into the car, in the commotion, the starfish broke into two parts. One part had three limbs and the other had two.

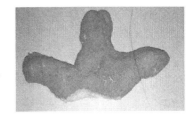

I had already begun driving by now. I crossed my fingers and started scheming how best to stem the flood of tears that was sure to come. To my surprise and delight, Sia paused, took a long look at the broken star fish and without any prompting or hesitation said, "The starfish is now a sailboat." Sallie the starfish had become Sal the sailboat!

I was both relieved and impressed. I later dissected her response, and this is what I believe her little brain went through in about ten seconds:

- She saw the broken starfish for what it was—a broken starfish (alternate response—blame dad for ruining her creation or spend time wishing it did not break)
- She accepted that her creation had broken and she won't be able to show it to others (alternate response—cry, throw a tantrum)
- She found something meaningful in what was left (alternate response—throw the pieces in the garbage)

Maybe I am reading too much into it. Maybe she didn't really care about the starfish as much as I thought she did. The lesson I learned was this: Make the best starfish you can, but if it breaks, then within the broken parts, find your sailboat. To me that is resilience.

Resilience Stories

In our journey together in this book, I will share many more stories of resilience. Inspiring stories often take birth in adversities. Resilience needs hardships and hurts to polish away the scratches and dirt off the human mind.

The chaos of trauma spawns stories—of men and women risking their lives to save victims of bomb blasts, of ordinary citizens saving strangers trapped beneath mounds of concrete brought down by an earthquake, of health workers risking it all to save lives of citizens in epidemic hit areas, of women physically blemished by chemical attacks who choose to show the beauty of their spirit rather than hide in dark basements, of someone scarred by third degree burns and paralyzed from waist down who chooses to be happy inside and share his happiness even though his face can't physically smile. Hats off to all these men and women who remind us of the tallest heights that human will and values can soar.

Your World

Perhaps the best way to think about resilience is to find it in your own world—the world that is alive around you today or the one saved in photo albums, or the memory networks of your brain. Think of someone in your personal life, who has had a lot of rough and tumble but is still standing strong and tall. Nobody can beat this person's spirit or love of life. This person is filled with hope, courage, and inspiration. He or she could be your friend, grandmother, spouse, child, sibling, neighbor, client, or someone else. That person is resilient.

Write a few lines about one such person in your life. Write his or her name, relationship with you, a resilience story, and in your view, what makes that person resilient.

Name: _____

Relationship: _____

A resilience story:

_____

_____

_____

What makes him/her resilient:

_____

_____

_____

Bring fond memories of this person to your mind for a few minutes, before reading further.

Having proposed that resilience is best understood as stories not definitions, let's still try to define it. We will pick not one, but three different definitions. I'll then track its journey over the last six decades. Just an FYI that this is the most technical chapter in the book.

2. Let's Define it Anyway

Here are the three of my favorite definitions of resilience:

1. Resilience is the core strength you use to lift the load of life.

2. Resilience is doing well when you shouldn't be doing well.

3. Resilience is your ability to withstand adversity (Resist), bounce back from adversity (Recover), and grow despite life's downturns (Rise).

Pick the definition that you like the best. It doesn't matter which one you pick because they all point in the same direction. I use the first definition when I am talking to entrepreneurs, college students, and others at the highest risk of energy depletion and burnout. The second definition is most useful when talking to patients and people who are stuck in difficult life situations. I find the third definition most useful in scientific communities. That's where we will start.

Scientific Definitions

Resilience has as many scientific definitions as there are experts defining it. Scientists have developed over a dozen scales to measure resilience.[17,18] Perusing through a few definitions will give you a flavor of the current thinking.[19,20] Resilience in material science refers to the capacity of a strained body to recover its size and shape after compressive stress deformation. It is the property of a material to absorb energy when it is deformed elastically and then, upon unloading, to have this energy recovered. The American Heritage Dictionary [2000] defines resilience as the ability to recover quickly from illness, change, or misfortune.

A few well-known definitions offered by psychologists are:
*   The personal qualities that enable one to thrive in the face of adversity.[21]
*   Positive patterns of adaptation in the context of adversity.[22]
*   The positive pole of individual differences in people's response to stress and adversity.[23]

Most definitions and scales use different words to describe the ability to cope with or adapt to challenges and bounce back from adversity.

Just as adversities can have countless faces, resilience also has countless forms. Resilience to acute adversity is different from resilience to long-term stressors. Resilience in children isn't the same as that in adults. Resilience in elderly often describes physiological reserve—their ability to preserve their functioning and independence despite illness, injury, or other insults.[24]

The same resilience at any age or in any form can be seen from three different perspectives—as trait, process, and outcome.

Being versus Becoming

Some people are born strong. Nothing seems to faze their willpower. They won the resilience lottery. Others take their time to find and develop that strength. Researchers thus look at resilience from a continuum of perspectives: capacity, process, and outcome.

Resilience as a capacity (called as trait) is someone's inherent build or characteristics that help them be strong. Specific personality traits are associated with a can-do attitude and greater ability to adapt. The key ingredients in an individual to such strength is the right genes and optimally wired brain.[25]

Resilience as a process describes the evolution of resilience through the interaction between individuals (their brain and body) and the totality of their environment—physical, biological, and societal.[26]

Resilience as an outcome is what ultimately happens to people as a consequence of the adversity. It is natural for most of us to initially feel overwhelmed when facing a health scare, narcissistic supervisor, or threat of bankruptcy. The key is what happens next. Do we collapse, get overwhelmed, or worse suicidal? Or do we recover, transform, take charge, become the change agent, and experience post-traumatic growth.[27,28]

Perhaps resilience is all three—core inner strength, a process and plan to recover, and thriving despite adversity as the ultimate outcome. You might notice that we don't define resilience as doing well when we should be doing well. Perhaps we should, because some of us are phenomenally skilled at making ourselves miserable, even in good times.

Nevertheless, resilience needs adversity to define it. Let's explore that next.

The Value of Adversity

Can you call someone resilient who is doing well but hasn't been challenged for a long time? Most experts agree that resilience isn't just feeling strong when unchallenged; resilience is radiating strength even through facing adversity. Resilience emerges in response to hardships.

The resilient response thus needs two components—a threat occurred + system adapted positively to the threat. The reason physicians perform stress tests of the heart to diagnose blocked arteries is because we can't predict, at rest, what will happen to the heart with exercise. Similarly, how a person is doing in good times cannot predict how he or she will respond to adversity.

Threat + Strength = Resilient Response

A person I know is extremely social, gregarious, fast talking, and charming. However, when criticized or concerned about failure, he completely collapses—he can't sleep, gets anxious, and starts lashing out at others. When you meet him at a party entertaining a group, in no way can you tell that he will crater so badly when challenged.

On the other hand, my friend told me a story about her mother, a petite woman in her sixties. She fell down while grocery shopping and sprained her ankle. Her family was hosting a dinner that night. She wrapped her ankle, took two ibuprofens and ran the whole show, not letting anyone know about her fall. After all the guests had left and dishes were done, she paused to look at her now severely hurting foot. It was puffed up twice its original size and was bluer than blueberry. An urgent x-ray showed she had fractured her ankle bone.

Where do people find such will? An exploration into resilience research will be a good first step to glean some insights.

3. Resilience Research

The Origins

The word resilience comes from the Latin word *resalire*, which means to bounce back or jump again. Physical scientists used this word to describe property of materials that help them spring back to the original form after deformity. In the 1970s and 1980s two fields adopted this idea—ecology and psychology.

Ecology describes resilience as the property of biological systems that helps them withstand and bounce back from natural or human influences that threaten those systems. Ecologists call resilience the ability to maintain structure, function and growth, and speed of recovery. An excellent example is coral reef colonies and how they survive bleaching.

Most coral reef colonies live with zooxanthellae that are single-celled organisms which provide carbohydrates to the corals and in turn are protected and nourished by the corals. Stress, related to changes such as increase in water temperature, salinity, pollution or acidification, breaks this relationship, leading to expulsion of zooxanthellae, which can eventually lead to death of the coral. Resilient coral communities are better able to resist the environmental forces that cause bleaching and find ways to survive if bleaching does happen. This is one among countless examples of resilience in nature.

Some of the earliest descriptions of resilience in humans were by Norman Garmezy who reported on a subset of patients with schizophrenia who were doing well compared to others.[29,30] Dr. Garmezy, or Norm as he was affably called by his colleagues, found that these "atypical schizophrenics" had better social relations, work history, marriage, and had greater capacity to fulfill responsibilities prior to the diagnosis. Somehow this better functioning baseline protected them from the worst effects of the illness.

Resilience in Children

The early descriptions of Garmezy among patients with schizophrenia were followed by a series of observations—by Werner's team in Kauai, Hawaii, by Garmezy's team that studied children of mothers with schizophrenia, and by Michael Rutter's team that studied children in inner city London and Isle of Wight. Although the numbers and predictors varied depending on the study, the headlines were the same—wherever researchers looked, to their surprise, they found a considerable proportion of children doing well when they shouldn't have been doing well. Repeatedly, researchers found three set of factors I mentioned earlier that helped children develop resilience: individual characteristics, families, and a wider social environment.

One story I found particularly striking (described by Swiss researcher Manfred Bleuler) was that of a 14-year-old girl whose father was an alcoholic and whose mother spent most of her time in the hospital because of a mental illness. This little girl raised four siblings, took care of her father, later married, had two kids and lived a fulfilling and content life. Parental neglect and illness couldn't touch her. Like the lotus that remains unspoilt by the muddy water; if anything adversity made her stronger.

Over the past several decades, several other groups have studied a variety of vulnerabilities with the goal of finding protective factors. Through everything from maltreatment,[31] poverty and community violence,[32,33] tragic experiences,[34-36] and chronic illness[37]—everywhere researchers have looked, they have found evidence of thriving.

As the resilience research evolved and matured in children, experts identified four waves of this research, each wave riding on top of the other.[22,38]

- The first wave described the concept of resilience and characteristics of people who thrive in the face of adversity.
- The second wave described the processes and mechanisms that allow resilience to blossom.
- The third wave focused on enhancing resilience through interventions and prevention.
- The fourth and most current wave integrates different disciplines such as neuroscience, genetics and endocrinology, looks for interaction between genes and environment, and tries to better understand resilience across species and disciplines.

All the four waves are still alive as we continue to refine and deepen our understanding.

Resilience in Adults

With time, expansion of resilience to adults was inevitable, due to rising stress levels in our society (from urbanization and other factors)[39] and better understanding of the adverse effect of stress on our physical, psychological, social, and occupational wellbeing. Initially, researchers followed children with adversities into adulthood and reported on resiliency outcomes after prolonged childhood trauma.[40,41] Both promotive and protective factors were found to continue into adulthood.[42]

Post 9/11 and the resulting unfortunate wars, a different line of research emerged. This involved studying resilience around major adversities such as wars, terrorism, and other traumatic events. A series of studies led by multiple teams showed, that just like in children, in adults, resilience trajectory was the most common outcome following a variety of traumas including 9/11, campus shootings, the loss of a spouse or partner, traumatic injury, medical procedures, military deployment,[43-45] and spinal cord injury.[27,46-48]

More recently, resiliency has expanded to include chronic stressors in adults—such as that of illness, overwork, relationship strain, caregiving, and more. Most of these studies aren't longitudinal; they assess stress and wellbeing measures at a particular point in time. Nevertheless, this cross-sectional data reveals high to very high levels of stress in a number of populations such as people with chronic pain, cancer survivors, heart disease, as well as professionals in several industries including health care, teaching, law, journalism, and most of the corporate world. Given that acute conditions aren't predictable and chronic conditions account for the majority of health care costs and societal stress, it is in helping adults with chronic long-term stressors that resilience research and interventions might offer the greatest societal benefit.[49]

Looking Past the Horizon

I think as resilience evolves, its scope will broaden. We will learn that resilience isn't just doing well when we <u>shouldn't</u> be doing well, but it is also doing well when we <u>should be</u> doing well. This is because most humans struggle with a brain that is wonderful at manufacturing pain.[50] We have a phenomenal ability to hurt ourselves with our imaginations and inventions. One part of resilience is not only to recover positive emotions in adversity, but also sustain contentment and joy when everything is going well.

Another way resilience will expand is into the prevention science. Resilience will grow to include our ability to preempt and prevent adversity. When you are fully aware and attentive, you become more effective at anticipating. A good driver is not only aware of his car but is also prepared for the mistakes others are likely to commit.

Eventually we will reach a point where resilience training will be as important for helping patients, professionals and students, as antibiotics, work-related skills, or core academic curriculum. Physicians are increasingly realizing that pharmacotherapy-focused medicine is increasing patient burden.[51] At some point we have to focus on building individual capacity so patients can better handle their illness. Similarly, professionals are experiencing high level of burnout, partly because of imbalance in demand and resources, lack of control, and lack of meaning. Helping them with emotional resilience is critical for them to adapt to the anticipated and accelerating changes.

Sadly, our students are also experiencing high level of burnout. Half of the medical students get burnt out before they complete medical school. Bolstering their resilience will be essential to create a vibrant and energized workforce of the future.

Your Thoughts

The purpose of the perspectives and research I have shared so far is for you to develop your own personal way of describing resilience. What makes the most sense to you? What is your preferred way of describing or defining resilience?

_____

_____

_____

Revisit your description above after you finish reading this book. Pen your refined thoughts and additional perspectives in the space below.

_____

_____

_____

When defining resilience, one question I am often asked is this—What (if any) is the difference between resilience and stress management? Are they synonyms, incremental, or completely different constructs? Let's explore this question next.

4. Resilience versus Stress Management

I have a close relative who is phenomenally skilled at pushing my buttons. I am sure I have my set of imperfections, but he has helped me feel unworthy and incompetent, more than I believe I deserve. This is one of those relationships that I can't get out of. Earlier I would endure his presence, and once he left, would lick my wounds and apply whatever balm was available at arm's length—a funny movie, calorie-dense food, shopping spree, time with friends, deep breathing—anything I could think of. All of these helped me rebalance and continue on with life. I see these as stress management skills.

As my perspectives developed and skills broadened, I thought there must be a better way I could walk away with just a graze and not a deep wound. I tried to understand him better. I learned about his difficult childhood, the abuse and rejections he had to endure, his insecurities, the medical conditions he is struggling with. I also worked on damping my buttons. All of this gave me new tools—compassion for his struggles, gratitude for what is right about him, acceptance of his and my imperfections, forgiveness, and openness to vulnerability. Now I prep myself with these tools before I meet him. I am happy to report that I have met him several times since, for days together, and have walked away without even a graze. In the process, I have learned things I wasn't doing right. I see these as resilience skills.

Resilience and stress management are overlapping concepts. However, considering them as distinct entities can help our understanding at this stage of exploration. You can understand the differences from three perspectives—time frame, reactive versus proactive, and recovery versus growth.

Time Frame

Stress management is looking through the rear-view mirror while resilience is gazing through the wind shield. From timeframe perspective, your life can be divided into two time zones—from the day of your birth until this moment, and from this moment until your last day.

Stress management is better handling all that happened until this moment, while resilience is preparing yourself for the rest of today, tomorrow and beyond. When I recover from the insult of a rude email, I am handling stress; when I prepare for the meeting tomorrow, I am enhancing my resilience.

Reactive versus Proactive

As an extension of above, stress management is reactive—reacting to what you have already got; while resilience is proactive—preparing for what is to come.

In most situations, stress management approaches take count of the stressors and generate a strategy to better handle them. Resilience skills are preventative and thus are applicable irrespective of the stressor. The palm trees in Florida don't know which hurricane season will bring the big one. These trees don't strengthen their roots the night of the storm. They work all year round so they are better prepared. Similarly for us, an adversity that can turn our life upside down is just an email or a phone call away. We can't predict the particular moment that will bring the giant tidal wave. Resilience helps you develop strong roots, so you don't crater.

Resilience also helps you when no adversity is around, because we humans don't need adversity to feel miserable; fear of the storm or memory of the previous storm can cause as much pain as the storm itself. When you are better at handling your emotions and are skilled at dodging the daily drain of negative emotions, you will be better prepared for that inevitable storm surge that arrives at some point in life for most of us.

Recovery versus Growth

With stress management you try to recover what you lost, with resilience you grow possibilities that didn't exist.

Stress management brings you back to the baseline; resilience helps lift you above the baseline, so your entire life is enhanced for the better. For example, after a physical illness, you try to recover and come back to your usual health. But when you take good care of yourself—with a healthy diet, exercise, sleep, and preventive care—you become stronger and do not fall sick as often. This applies not only for the physical body, but for every aspect of your life.

The three ideas presented above can be summarized in the figure below:

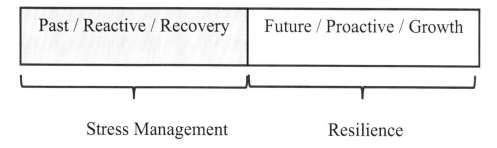

| Past / Reactive / Recovery | Future / Proactive / Growth |

Stress Management   Resilience

I must re-emphasize that the dichotomy I have suggested above is mainly for understanding. In reality the set of skills that decrease your stress also enhance your resilience, and enhancing resilience brings down the stress level. In research studies resilience and stress almost always move in the opposite direction.[52-54]

With this background understanding, we'll now move into exploring different facets of resilience—we will search for resilience in nature, see how vulnerability can actually be a resilience factor, break down resilience into four core domains, find how resiliency relates to your genetic makeup, explore the core outcome of gene and environment interaction—a resilient mindset, and find unique ways in which you are resilient. I'll focus only on the details that matter, where the rubber meets the road, and not get into the minutiae of every research study. At places I will spend a few paragraphs on scientific details. I hope you will enjoy learning how the resilience field is moving forward. Feel free to skip or skim anytime I wander into nerd-land.

Let's start with nature.

5. Three Examples from Nature

One of the best ways to understand life is to look deeper into nature. Nature offers several unique advantages. Once you come to love nature, you can have a love affair of a lifetime, with no fear of rejection. You can be yourself in nature, even on a bad hair day. Nature also offers tremendous variety. What can be more musical than the chirpings that announce the sunrise, more gorgeous than a blooming hibiscus, and more inspiring than the migration of monarchs?

Trees can also teach us a lot about resilience. They have been around for about four hundred million years. They know how to adapt, bounce back and grow because of adversity. Despite being stationary and vulnerable—to storms, droughts, beetles, elephants, and more—they have thrived. Here are three that have taught me a lot about resilience.

The Mango Tree

I grew up picking ripe sweet mangoes in our neighborhoods and farms. We lived in very hot humid tropical climate where mercury would routinely touch 110 degrees Fahrenheit. We tolerated the singeing heat because of one reason—we knew that the hotter it got, the riper and sweeter the mangoes became. Some of my fondest memories of childhood are the six of us (me and my three siblings and our parents), sitting around a bucket full of mangoes, eating till we got short of breath from our diaphragm pushing on our lungs.

Mangos don't burn from the hot sun. They ripen and sweeten with heat. The lesson—when exposed to heat, ripen don't burnout.

The Bamboo

Bamboo is a grass that can grow taller than 150 feet. Unlike most trees, a bamboo stem is as broad near the tip as it is at the base. The stem has to withstand strong compressive forces and has thus evolved to be stronger than concrete. Mostly hollow and thus very light, the stem sways with the wind. It has thus evolved to be supple too. Because of the peculiarity of arrangement of its fibers, the stem is stronger than steel in its resistance to being pulled apart. Further, the density of fibers helps it bend without snapping. This unique combination of flexibility and strength is the reason bamboo has historically been the primary skeleton for homes and other hardy structures in many parts of the world.

Bamboo has other features too that make it resilient. High silica content makes it resistant to termites. It also has the highest growth rate among any plant. Bamboo can grow as fast as three feet in a day. Further, even after the stem is harvested, the root system remains connected to each other, keeping the soil together, and giving rise to the next generation of stems.

Bamboo teaches us that strength coupled with flexibility can make you very resilient, and in turn, very useful. The lesson—bend so you do not break.

The Willow

We have several willow trees in our neighborhood. For some reason, they love the cold Midwest. I wish I could claim that while shoveling snow in May.

Willow trees have evolved to reach the perfect arrangement to be able to survive the windy plains. They have flexible branches and strong roots. The branches are long and bending. They may look weak, but in a storm, they twist and turn and don't easily snap. At the same time, the trees have very strong root systems that extend far beyond their canopy. Willow roots can extend up to one hundred feet beyond the center of the trunk. As a result, willow trees are often the last ones standing in high winds.

Extrapolating to our lives, flexible branches correlate with flexible preferences, while strong roots correlate with strong principles. It helps to be flexible and strong at the right places. Be flexible about minor details like what is for dinner or on which side of the bed you sleep. But be strong in your principles such as integrity and commitment. Your flexibility about the trivial saves you the energy to be strong about the real important.

The lesson—be flexible about the preferences and strong about the principles.

Mango, bamboo and willow offer three among countless examples of resilience in nature. Resiliency and its outcome of survival emerges in very many unique ways. In fact, you'll be surprised that at times even vulnerability can be a resilience factor. Let's talk about that next.

6. How Vulnerability Can Make Us Resilient

Biologically among animals, a resilience factor works in two ways, it:

- Helps them avoid illness, injury or starvation (the most resilient animals die of old age), and
- Helps them reproduce to maintain their clan.

Sometimes, vulnerability can unexpectedly confer resilience, especially if that vulnerability provides serendipitous protection from an even more ominous threat. Let me share one such fascinating example.

Sickle Cells

A blood disorder common in some populations is sickle cell anemia. This is the first medical condition that was described because of a specific genetic modification (mutation). This mutation affects the production of hemoglobin, the oxygen carrying molecule in red blood cells. Individuals need two copies of the mutation (one each from mom and dad) to develop the full-blown illness.

In this disease hemoglobin in red blood cells tends to clump, particularly when patients are exposed to dehydration, low oxygen, infection, or other stressful situations. Clumping causes the cells to assume abnormal shapes (classically sickle shape). These cells then block the narrow capillaries in the body. As a result the cells die sooner, and the person develops blocked blood vessels, resulting in a devastating chronic illness that causes pain, organ damage, life-long disability, and early death.

Most inherited illnesses that cause early death tend to have low prevalence because not many people with these illnesses live long enough to reproduce and pass on their genes. To the surprise of many scientists, sickle cell disease was an exception. Its prevalence was as high as 10 to 40 percent in some areas of the world. Why?

Turns out these were the very areas that had the highest prevalence of another life-threatening condition—malaria.

A form of malaria called falciparum malaria is particularly sinister. The parasite causing this illness invades red blood cells, destroying them in the process, resulting in anemia and severe damage to many different organs. Malaria was a devastating illness in older times and still is, in many parts of the world. It was perhaps the single biggest cause of early death for our ancestors, particularly during the agricultural period. Even now, about 200 million people get malaria every year.

Now, what if you have a genetic condition that protects you from malaria, particularly the worst kind? Won't that genetic condition increase your chance of survival? That's where the sickle cell story gets interesting. Research shows that malarial parasites don't like to infect sickle cells. Further, patients with sickle cell anemia have a favorable biochemical and immune response that protects them from the worst form of malaria, called the cerebral malaria. While this all sounds good for the patients with sickle cell anemia, it might not make a significant dent on their survival, especially if the underlying cause of anemia was uniformly fatal (if they survive malaria, they are taken down by the sickle cell).

So, the next question is---could there be a benign form of sickle cell anemia where people are expected to live for long, but not get the malaria? Interestingly, that is precisely the case. A subset of people with sickle cell inherit only one abnormal gene from either parent. They develop what is called sickle cell trait which is not as devastating. Some conditions are actually very mild with minimal to no effect on longevity. Nevertheless, they are still 60 percent less likely to die of falciparum malaria compared to people with normal hemoglobin.

Do you see how a genetic abnormality can actually serve as a protective factor, even help save one's life? Having sickle cell was thus a resilience factor in older times, as it still is in the parts of the world where malaria is rampant.

Sickle cell is just one example. Several other mutations, some known and many unknown, confer protection from a variety of illnesses. One of them that got popular recently is the mutation that protects us from the worst form of the HIV infection.[55] The key to protection is that the mutation itself doesn't cause devastating harm and the illness that the mutation is protecting you from could be a significant cause of disability and death.

If the illness isn't a cause of severe disability or death, then the mutation will have limited benefits. For example, if a mutation today decreases your chance of mild acne, myopia or dental caries by 90 percent, it will be of limited survival value compared to one that decreases your chance of heart attack by even 10 percent. The same mutation for acne will be of material value if acne becomes a major cause of human mortality. A mutation that prevents dental caries will definitely help female lions who start losing their teeth in old age, affecting their hunting capacity. Similarly, the myopia gene would be catastrophic for bald eagles.

I hope the above examples helped you see how dynamic and fascinating is the emergence of resilience. Sometimes it can also be unpredictable, with good genes making you vulnerable and bad genes protecting you in ways you couldn't have imagined. Funny, isn't it!

Broadly, resilience emerges from an interaction between adversity and physical/psychological/social/environmental response to that adversity. Your response relates to four individual attributes that span the domain of physical, cognitive, emotional, and spiritual aspects. Let's explore them next.

7. The Four Domains

Like the four wheels of an automobile that collaborate and not compete, resilience has four collaborating domains—physical, cognitive, emotional, and spiritual.

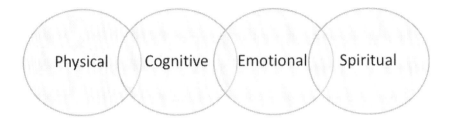

Physical Resilience

Perhaps you have taken a stress test of your heart. In a stress test, the technician gradually increases speed and incline while monitoring your pulse, blood pressure, symptoms, and electrocardiogram. He or she evaluates how far you can go before you can't go further, how quickly you recover back to baseline, and how your EKG, blood pressure, and other parameters change. Every one of us will eventually have to stop. You can't run like a cheetah or climb like a mountain goat. With respect to the stress test, physical resilience has two parts—going as far or farther than what is predicted for someone your age (Resist) and recovering quickly back to baseline (Recover). To this you can add having no concerning symptoms, an unexpected EKG, pulse, or blood pressure changes.

You can extrapolate this model to different body organs/organ systems, such as your lungs, kidneys, intestines, immune system, and other systems. Of course, the specific stressor and definition of recovery will be different for each organ. For the intestines it might be how well they can handle the 4000-calorie Thanksgiving dinner, for the kidneys it might be how well they can handle the sodium chloride of four extra salty pretzels, and for the immune system it might be how well it can handle a large dose of viruses from a stranger's unguarded sneeze.

A useful construct here is that of reserve. We can lose 80 percent of the intestines and still continue to absorb food. Patients with kidneys working only at 20 percent of their capacity often do not need dialysis. Heart, liver, blood cells—most of our body's systems have built in reserves. Good reserves translate into feeling robust (for your age), falling sick less often, and recovering quickly from an illness.

The whole-person physical resilience emerges from resilience at the molecular, genetic, cellular, tissue, and organ levels. This depends on three core variables—your genetic make-up, your environment, and the choices you make. You have little control over the genes you inherited, only partial control over your environment, but a whole lot of control over your choices. Good (or bad) genes definitely can make a difference, but 50 percent of your wellbeing depends on the choices you make. In fact, the number one cause of premature deaths in the U.S. is our inability to make and stick with good choices.[56]

Aerobic exercise, good sleep, and a healthy diet are perhaps the three most important components of a healthy lifestyle. They also enhance your happiness[57-63] and the health of your brain.[64-67] Optimal preventive care and seeking competent medical care when needed is also very important. Before you feel guilty, however, it might be comforting to know that less than five percent of us are exercising all the healthy choices. The good news is our body doesn't expect for you to be perfect; good enough will do. Striving for perfection can actually be counterproductive. Often, if we aim for perfection and aren't able to achieve it, we give up all together.

If you aren't sure where to start, here are two simple suggestions—avoid prolonged sitting and get to bed on time. A considerable proportion of us are good about going to the gym but will then sit for four or six hours at a stretch before getting up. We also overcommit or overindulge and then get to bed at 2 AM, day after day after day. Prolonged sitting undoes many of the benefits of exercise. Inadequate sleep is as bad as any other major stressor in life.

Both, physical activity and good sleep help with the next domain—cognitive resilience.

Cognitive Resilience

Have you said something you later regretted? Honked at cars out of frustration? Blanked on your password? Struggled with a name? Choked or panicked at a presentation? If yes, you have experienced the limits of human cognitive resilience.

Our three core cognitive functions are attention, memory, and judgment/decision making. Cognitive resilience is your ability to preserve these abilities in the middle of a stressful situation. The relationship between stress and cognitive functions isn't linear; it follows an inverted U curve.

Too little stress is boring and counterproductive to work or fulfilling life. As the stress goes up, your focus and memory improve. You reach an optimal level of stress that motivates and challenges you. Beyond this level, downslope starts. Your focus and memory degrade until you reach a panic point. Cognitive resilience helps broaden your optimal zone, so you aren't bored as often and don't panic as easily. Let's look at each of the three core cognitive functions, how stress affects them, and how resilience can make a difference.

Attention is the gateway into your mind. Excessive stress affects your attention in two ways. First, it tunnels your attention, so your focus zeroes on only what is immediately in front of you (Think about rushing through airport security while your flight has started boarding. You might not notice people in front of or behind you). Nature designed it this way so in duress, we prioritize evaluating only the immediately relevant information that is likely of survival value. This is good for a hundred-meter sprint or when running away from a grizzly; but not so good when giving a talk or negotiating a contract. Second, excessive stress biases our attention to the threatening. We become exquisitely sensitive to sound, images, or memory of the fearful. This predisposition wreaks havoc in people with post-traumatic stress disorder (PTSD). It also hurts our relationships, when we can't see the good intentions in our partner, friends, or colleagues.

Cognitive resilience helps you preserve your focus, so your attention isn't as tunneled. You are still able to process complexity. Further, while you pay attention to the fearful, you process it in its fuller context, and are thus not as reactive. Preserving your attention is very important to succeeding in both personal and professional life.

Memory is your ability to code, store, and retrieve information. Excessive stress causes nerve cell loss in one of the most important memory areas of the brain—hippocampus. Stress has a constricting effect on memory; because of this effect, we start focusing on the most recently available information. Stress also decreases working memory capacity (working memory is like RAM in your computer; it helps you temporarily store information). Impairment of working memory interferes with your ability to hold and process information.

Like attention, the constricting effect on memory would be helpful for immediate physical threats. However, you will become less effective in integrating the past and present to guide your future. You will also perform poorly in complex negotiations, be it negotiating a raise with your supervisor or convincing your teenager to eat five servings of fruits and vegetables each day.

Resilience helps preserve your memory so you can better handle complex issues and also have a greater bandwidth to sift through multiple pieces of information. When stuck in a difficult situation, resilience helps you think through the details more clearly and maintain your balance and sense of humor.

Judgment/decision making is your ability to integrate your personal goals and motivation with information from attention and memory and translate the resulting insight to a rational view of life and the world. Excessive stress hurts this process in every way. Stress decreases the number of choices available to your mind and delays disengagement from failing alternatives. It switches you into survival mode. You lose self-control and are more likely to make irrational, unhealthy choices. My favorite drug for excessive stress is a stat dose of a chocolate chip cookie. Bigger the better.

Have you sometimes surprised yourself by making a very irrational decision? Every time you tell yourself, what was I thinking, you were likely in the throes of excessive stress. No wonder scientists use the blunt catchphrase—stress makes us stupid.

Resilience preserves the activity of your higher cortical brain, so that your higher brain areas fully participate in judgment and decision making. The higher cortical brain also reins in the fear evoking part of the brain (amygdala). With the amygdala in check, you will likely say and do fewer things that could get you in trouble.

Your attention, memory, judgment and decision making depend on keeping a healthy brain. Multiple research studies show that different elements of cognitive resilience are helped by aerobic exercise, a healthy diet (and weight), restorative sleep, ongoing mental stimulation, openness to experience, social support, social activity, and good motivation.

Cognitive resilience is intimately related to and depends on emotional resilience.

Emotional Resilience

Do you sometimes wake up feeling blah for no reason? Do you have a colleague, friend or loved one whose mood swings are unpredictable? Do you feel like you are walking on eggshells with someone in your life? Do you dread giving negative news to someone, fearful that he or she will overreact? Do you know someone who stews on a minor negative experience for days, weeks, or months? All these are examples of deficits in emotional resilience.

Emotional resilience has two parts: experiencing positive emotions and recovering quickly from negative emotions. Emotional resilience doesn't mean not experiencing negative emotions. It isn't Pollyanna. Instead, emotional resilience is emotional balance. Negative emotions are protective and in small doses and in combination with positive emotions are a healthy part of our emotional portfolio.

Emotionally resilient people use their emotional energy to serve their life's meaning. They are mindful of their emotions and know when to discipline their emotional voice so a mistake doesn't become a catastrophe, as happens so often these days in countless modern examples of rage (road rage, flight rage, work rage, vending machine rage...).

Here are seven elements of emotional resilience:

#1. Be willing to see the bad: Emotionally resilient people do not close their eyes to the truth. They do not avoid looking at fears. They know that running away from fears increases the grip of fears in their life. They are willing to look at fear in its face. They don't routinely get anxious with low cellphone battery. They are also willing to experience the full repertoire of emotions, albeit setting boundaries, so they do not let the bad define their day.

#2. See the bad as not so bad: Anytime I feel low, all I have to do is take a walk across the hospital campus. A sight of little kids in wheelchairs and of young people walking with walkers shakes me to the core and reminds me that what I am calling bad is truly trivial in comparison to what others are going through. Emotional resilience helps you take the bad in perspective of how bad it could have been, but isn't. That awareness will evoke both gratitude and compassion.

#3. See that the bad is just one part of life: When a close loved one was struggling with food allergies, we sat down to make a list of all she could eat. We discovered that apples come in 7500 varieties, and bananas in 1500. The list of what she could still eat was a mile long. She realized that she literally had millions of options to choose from. This zooming out gave her the perspective. Experiencing the bad, we can either focus on just the bad, or use the bad as a reminder about all that is good. To me that is a good way of practicing gratitude.

#4. See that the bad is limited in time: The expression, "this too shall pass," comes from a place of wisdom. The snow on the sidewalk finally melts, memory of the hurt eventually fades, a bad year eventually ends, kids finally grow out of diapers, slow internet eventually becomes faster. The last one isn't guaranteed. Like the good, the bad thankfully has an expiration date. Though it may seem to live longer than desirable, the bad is limited in time and scope. If you choose to lift the load of only the next one hour, it may become more bearable.

#5. See that you aren't alone in facing the bad: Currently, 80 percent of us experience excessive stress, two out of three feel daily discrimination, one out of two will experience or see a catastrophic event…We could continue counting numbers. Here is the truth. We are together in our suffering. Though the details and depth may be different, we all have to bear our share of pain and agony. All of this evolves over a period of time. The good times in someone's life today will cycle into the not so good times before they know it. A friend once told me a story of a couple that lived a high life. When invited for dinner the wife said, "We have too many friends. We can't afford to invest time in anyone else." That was then. A few years later, her husband died in an airline crash. Her financial situation worsened. Most of her friends walked away. She was now hungry for a kind ear. Instead of developing hubris in the good times, it might be best to keep a humble disposition, knowing that you and everyone else will have your share of sorrows and joy. Savor the good times, learn from the bad times, and keep compassion for those who you see are struggling.

#6. Is it really bad? Thousands of us are alive today because we missed a flight, took a wrong turn, or decided to leave the building for a cup of tea. I have met several people who were stuck in bad relationships, only to realize later how that relationship saved them from somebody or something else that could have been much worse. Sometimes the adversity today saves us from a catastrophe tomorrow. It is good to consider that possibility, because it might provide you the meaning you need to stop calling bad as bad. Maybe the bad is actually good but the effects will play out over the long term.

#7. Think about your strengths, not just vulnerabilities: One diagnosis that creates the greatest dread among patients is cancer. They cannot imagine how they will face the rigors of chemotherapy, radiation, and surgery, and then the fear of recurrence. Most patients who have to face this unfortunate diagnosis do better than they could have imagined. Support comes from all corners—work colleagues, friends, neighbors, and of course, loved ones. They find inner emotional strength, often get more spiritual, and start focusing on what is most important in their life. For those who are cured of the cancer, many in retrospect consider the diagnosis to be a gift that reset their values and life's direction.

With changing times, our anxieties are also evolving. Some of the modern-day concerns are uniquely 21st century. A few of these, some trivial and some more substantial, that I have personally experienced are fear of identity theft, missing a flight, losing cell phone contact, no retweets/republishes, low cellphone battery, getting tagged in embarrassing pictures, not getting tagged at all, typos in texts and posts, and more. I also dread placing a telephonic order for carryout in a low cellphone coverage area to an impatient vendor who is clearly having a bad day.

The truth is that you are stronger than you can ever imagine. Because you and I can't know or imagine our strengths, we put only our fears and vulnerabilities in the equation. Complete these two sentences to take a tally of your resources:

I have (list people and assets you have; use additional space if necessary):

_____

_____

_____

_____

I can (list your strengths/all you can do; use additional space if necessary):

_____

_____

_____

_____

Emotional resilience helps you take a more rational look. It helps you to be rationally optimistic. The reason I say rationally optimistic is because unbridled optimism isn't healthy. In fact, there are some situations where healthy pessimism is helpful. In situations where the cost of mistake could be very high, such as for neurosurgeons or airline pilots, thinking about and being prepared for all that could go wrong is better than being the deer in the headlights. On the other hand, when you have already taken the plunge and are seeking solutions for a difficult problem, optimism will help. Emotional resilience helps you recruit and balance both these perspectives depending on the need of the hour.

Such balance empowers you to experience the good in your life—meaning, laughter, and love. It also helps you develop greater hope, courage, and inspiration—an indomitable will that powers through difficult times and takes full advantage of the good times.

Spiritual Resilience

Have you sometimes looked at the sky wondering who we are after all? Have you meditated on a higher meaning behind all this, and if yes, what is that meaning? Have you thought about how are we related to each other and the other myriad species on the planet? Have you pondered over how this world came into existence and what will be its ultimate fate? None of these are fully answerable in the scientific realm. But perhaps the real growth isn't in answering; it is in asking and thinking about the answers.

Spiritual resilience is powering your life with higher meaning and an altruistic perspective. It is thinking thoughts, speaking words, and doing work that serves the collective. The emphasis is on "living" the principles rather than just reading or talking about them.

The core component of spiritual resilience is a belief in something larger than oneself. Spiritually resilient people have a strong sense of purpose. They believe in a reality that transcends their limited life span. The specifics of this belief may be many. They do not create silos, rigid rituals, or thrust their beliefs on others. They just humbly carry a hope-filled vision of the world, considering life as meaningful and each good thought, word and action as precious. This belief helps them remain humble in success and hopeful in adversity. It provides them the umbrella so they do not get soaked in downpour. They do not avoid the rain; they use the umbrella to tread through the monsoon that is life.

What is the key tool to cultivate spiritual resilience? It is developing deep thinking. Deep thought is a powerful force. If there is anything that has changed the world over the last several millennia, it is our capacity for sustained deep thinking. Deep thinking powers creative insights, and everything else that follows. Essential to deep thinking is being able to silence the noise inside your head. You can access that silence in many ways—meditation, prayer, music, singing, working out, painting, and more.

A belief in deeper meaning and the strong attention nurtured by deep thinking helps you develop persistence in your efforts. Persistence has great power. You can see the power of persistence in how the Colorado river has carved the mighty Grand Canyon over millions of years. Such is the power of spiritual resilience.

Going back to the four-wheel model (which is where we started our discussion here)—physical and cognitive resilience are the two front wheels, while emotional and spiritual resilience are the two rear wheels. I believe the human vehicle is a rear wheel drive. The front wheels, physical and cognitive aspects of your life, while more visible, are powered by the silent rear wheels, your emotions and your beliefs.

These four wheels are hosted and led by the most complex biological information processor built by nature that sits in our head—our brain. Our brain's layout is controlled by the microscopic genes within our cells. Let's explore some fascinating discoveries about how these four domains of resilience, particularly the emotional resilience, are coded in our genome.

8. Resiliency Genes

In this chapter I wish to convey two messages:

- Genes influence your resilience; and
- Resilience influences your genes.

Read on if you wish to go deeper into the scientific details.

Cellular Details
Here is genomics 101:

- The 50-70 trillion cells that make our physical body each have 46 chromosomes (there are a few exceptions, but let's not bother about them right now).
- Chromosomes are the homes of our genes.
- A gene is a recipe for different types of proteins, the main raw material that builds our body.
- We all have the same 20,000 genes (again there are a few exceptions, but we can ignore them for now).

From the foregoing, you might ask two questions:
#1 If we all have the same genes, what makes us so different from each other?
#2 If every cell of our body is endowed with the same genes, why do different cells (such as neurons, fibroblasts, and lymphocytes) look and behave so differently?

The essence of our query is to understand how nature creates variety. If nature hadn't figured out how to create variety, we would all be gelled together in one homogeneous soup of slime. Interestingly, it isn't about the number of chromosomes. For example, chimpanzees and potatoes have the same number of chromosomes, and more than humans—48. However, I am sure you'll agree that we live richer and more complex lives than potatoes.

Here are the three ways nature creates variety.

#1. Different versions: Although all of us humans have the same 20,000 genes, we have different versions of the same genes. Look at it as making a Lego toy with 20,000 blocks. Let's assume each block comes in four different colors. With that much variety you can create trillions of different arrangements. Each of these arrangements represents a unique individual.

#2. Differential activation: In an orchestra, not every instrument plays all the time. Same is true for the genes. The behavior of our cells at any moment depends not only on which genes we have, but also on which genes are turned on or off at any moment. This is regulated by switching genes that act like a conductor—turning some genes off and other genes on, just at the right time, depending on the prevailing needs and responsibilities of the cell.

#3. <u>Role of the environment</u>: There is truth to the statement that some people get beneath our skin. Every aspect of the physical world you live in and the psychological world you experience influences your genetic and cellular behavior. One word that describes the influence of the external world on our genes is epigenetics.

Epigenetics

The word epigenetics is a combination of epi, meaning upon and genetics, meaning the sequence of genes. In essence, it is the change in gene behavior without a change in gene sequence. A more complete scientific definition is, "the stably heritable phenotype resulting from changes in a chromosome without alterations in the DNA sequence."[68] If you aren't a geneticist, then you don't have to bother understanding that definition!

Just as you dress up for an occasion, our DNA also dresses up for our life's situations. A number of changes that do not touch the genetic sequence but changes the way how DNA is dressed up, changes the gene expression. These include DNA methylation, histone modification, and changes in secondary structures formed by DNA and histones.[69] Such changes are affected by a variety of experiences that range from toxic stress in childhood to neighborhood social environments.[70] The expressions of several genes involved in the stress response (BDNF, Glucocorticoid receptor, serotonin transporter, tyroxine hydroxylase) are affected by the stress response itself, creating a feedback loop.[71]

These changes accumulate during the lifetime of the cell and when cells divide, they can pass on these changes to the baby cells.[72] If the changes happen in the sperm and ovum, the changes get inherited by the offspring.[73-75] Thus acquired parental anxiety and depression as well as resilience can be transmitted to the next generation.[76,77] Isn't it interesting that nature has figured out ways so we aren't limited to the lineup of the genes we are born with?

50:50

Nature has ensured that we are a product of our biology, circumstances, and the choices we make. A useful rule of thumb is that about 50 percent (range 30-60 percent) of your resilience is related to your genetic endowment.[78,79] The rest depends on your life situation (~10 percent), and the choices you make (~40 percent). The choices are important because, to a large extent, they are in your control.

For example, altruistic thoughts and actions activate anti-inflammatory genes, while selfish thoughts and actions activate pro-inflammatory genes.[80] Physical exercise, a healthy diet, good sleep, positive relationships, a nurturing social life—all of these and more influence our genetic expression.[81-84] Since the collective wellbeing of each cell eventually influences our physical and emotional health, we can literally build our resilience by making the right choices.

These choices interact with our genetic makeup that experts call gene environment interaction (GxE).[85] One fascinating example of how genes interact with the environment (GxE) is worth studying to appreciate how nature and nurture work with each other.

One Resiliency Gene

Serotonin is a hormone and a neurotransmitter that has considerable effects on an individual's personality. Once serotonin is released by the nerve cell it is transported back through a protein (called 5-HTT). A specific gene encodes for this protein (SLC6A4). This gene can code for two types of the protein—the long form that is associated with higher expression and the short form with lower expression.

In a classic study reported in 2003, researchers found that in response to similar stressful life events, individuals who had the short form of the protein had more depressive symptoms and more frequent diagnosis of depression and suicidal thoughts compared to individuals who had the long form.[86] Several (but not all), follow up studies have confirmed these findings, specifically identifying neuroticism (proneness to negative emotions) as a mediator.[87] Research shows that inheritance of the short form of protein is associated with lower emotional resilience, as measured by standard resilience scales.[88] This is a classic example of how genes interact with environment to influence stress and resilience.[89,90]

The effect of this gene has been found not only in humans, but also in mice and monkeys.[91] Further, the effect is not only limited to feelings and behaviors, but also to the response of the pituitary, adrenal and other glands in stressful situations,[91,92] and alcohol dependence.[93] Even athletes who inherit the small form of the protein have been found to have a higher risk of anxiety and depressive symptoms.[94]

A Soup of Genes

If it was only one gene influencing our stress and resilience, life would be simpler. But, as you can guess, we have a number of genes that interact with each other and with the environment to influence our personality and behavior.[77,95-102]

Some examples include: MAO-A VNTR low activity variant, Norepinephrine transporter gene, alpha 2 adrenergic receptor gene, HTR 1 A variant, COMT VAL158Met polymorphism, NPY-gene, FKBP5 gene, CRHR1 gene, Dopamine receptor genes, BDNF Val66Met polymorphism, and the PHF21B gene.[103] [104-107] This soup is perhaps the reason why adversity 'sensitizes' some people, while it has a 'steeling' effect on others.[108]

One of the best understood way that genes affect our resilience is by influencing how different parts of the brain connect and talk to each other.[109,110] This is through changing the release of hormones, neurotransmitters, and nerve growth factors (together we will call them neurochemicals) and/or changing the receptors to which these chemicals attach. Let's explore the different chemicals that bathe your brain. A general knowledge about these chemicals will help you develop insight into the chemistry of angst and joy.

9. The Brain Chemistry

Our brain is a busy organ—it secures our safety and nourishment, is a life-long learner, helps us experience pleasure, takes care of others, runs work-related tasks, and remembers the ever-growing list of our user IDs and passwords. Some of its goals conflict with each other. We love calorie-dense food but also have to remain healthy; we love to spread our genes but are bound by social norms; we love money and fame but can't steal our way into wealth and popularity. Achieving all these goals for about eight decades is a momentous task, the biological basis of which is a combo of different neurochemicals that bathe our brain.

A key aspect of these neurochemicals is a balance in their levels, so no single neurotransmitter hijacks the entire brain for a long time. Consider the fireplace metaphor. You want the fire in the fireplace, but also want to keep the fire contained within the fireplace. You have to balance the forces that create the fire and the ones that contain it.

The same phenomenon happens in the brain. For each of its functions, our brain has chemicals that increase the function (accelerators) as well as decrease the same function (brakes). Some chemicals can do both the jobs depending on the part of the brain they are influencing (dual roles). Here we will evaluate the role of the chemicals with respect to the stress response.[111,112]

Accelerators

Accelerators fuel the stress response. They include norepinephrine, CRH and cortisol.

* Norepinephrine (NE) is the classic fight and flight hormone. It enhances alertness and vigilance, increases heart rate, releases glucose from energy stores, and increases blood flow to the muscles and the brain. NE also shifts the brain into the more instinctive mode, so the brain focuses more on what is in its front and is less capable of the more complex thought out responses (as in running away from the grizzly versus wondering why humans don't have fur).

* CRH release leads to arousal, motor activity, fear, and increased fear memory. Most importantly, CRH mediates the release of one of the key accelerators, cortisol.

* Cortisol acts slower than NE. It releases energy and replenishes energy stores. Cortisol also enhances focus, vigilance, attention to the threatening, and memory of the event. The effects of cortisol depend on the amount and for how long it is released. While acute release of cortisol is helpful, chronically elevated cortisol predisposes to loss of neurons in the memory area of the brain (hippocampus), depressive symptoms, elevated blood sugar, inflammation, inhibition of growth and reproduction, and immune suppression.

Brakes

Brakes slow down the stress response. They include neuropeptide Y, galanin, and DHEA.

* NPY slows the ongoing NE release so it doesn't overshoot. Studies in the military show that the more resilient members have higher NPY.[113,114] Further, administering NPY in the brains of mice or even spraying NPY in animal's noses has been shown to decrease the stress response; clinical trials in humans are under way.[115,116]

* Galanin also brakes NE release, thereby decreasing stress and anxiety like behavior. In addition, galanin promotes new neuron formation.

* DHEA helps with metabolism, is anti-inflammatory, and anti-oxidant. Higher level of DHEA protects from the adverse effects of cortisol. While the natural DHEA produced by the body has multiple benefits, giving it from the outside showed no significant benefits in clinical studies.[117] Another hormone, allopregnanolone, also turns down the CRH and cortisol release.

Dual Role

Chemicals with a dual role can fuel or douse the stress response, depending on where in the brain, how much is released, and what else is going on. They include dopamine, serotonin, and brain derived neurotrophic factor (BDNF).

* Dopamine is involved in motivation, attention, and behavior. Too much dopamine can cause cognitive impairment, but too little can keep fear activity going. Dopamine is the key hormone involved in the reward circuit that makes people crave chocolate chip cookies and success, as well as gambling and cocaine.

* Serotonin influences moods, wellbeing/happiness, and sleep. The precise effect of serotonin depends on which receptor is being stimulated in which part of the brain. It can decrease or increase anxiety. The physiology of serotonin is much too complex for us to explore further here.

* BDNF is one amongst a family of chemicals that help nerve cells branch, divide, and form new connections. BDNF in stress promoting areas of the brain (such as the amygdala) can increase the stress response, though the same chemical in stress braking areas of the brain (hippocampus and prefrontal cortex), helps with decreasing stress.

The above list is meant to be illustrative and not comprehensive. I am sure there are numerous other chemicals waiting to be discovered. Each of these chemicals and their receptors are affected by the genetic makeup of the person. Thus, person A with healthy NPY and DHEA in their system may have a lower stress response compared to person B who comes wired to dump lots of NE and cortisol into the fire. This realization will help you to be kinder to those who struggle with a predisposition to stress. In many instances they are not choosing to be this way; they came wired to generate adrenaline.

The take home message of the previous two chapters is that your genes influence your behavior by influencing the brain structure and function. Further, while your genes are important, they depend on your environment and the choices you make. If you are born into abject poverty in an abusive family, then your good genes will struggle. Your constraints, opportunities, and role models powerfully influence your strengths and weaknesses. All of these together carve the attitude you carry—your mindset.

10. Resilient Mindset

Your every thought, word and action can be interpreted in many different ways. You can call slow as lazy or deliberate, saving money as miser or prudent, going the extra mile as obsessive or committed, praise as pandering or appreciation, kindness as weakness or strength. It all depends on your mindset.

Mindset is a set of attitudes you carry. Your attitude depends on how you think about the world and its happenings. It turns out that there is a recipe for having a resilient mindset. Like a recipe for food, once you add the right ingredients and let it marinate for some time, the outcome can be a mind that helps you savor more and struggle less. Let's get to know these ingredients.

The Resilient People

In chapter 1, I asked you to think about someone in your life you find resilient. I have been asking this question for the last decade to a lot of people. The follow up question I often ask is—"What makes this person resilient?" Here are the three themes that have emerged.

- **The resilient people are "other centric."** The resilient people's life forces are directed to serve the collective. They become strong so they can lift the weight for others, they collect wealth so they can share, they become famous so they can make a difference. Their strength comes from the collective strength of those they serve. They like to help, they live to help, and in the process of helping others, they help themselves.

- **They choose good role models.** Resilient people learn from many, but they allow only the most inspiring people to enter their inner thoughts. They bypass negative influences quickly, using those examples to learn what not to do, just like the resilient children did in Kauai, Hawaii.

- **They carry an inspired hopeful construct of the world.** The resilient people cling to hope in despair, courage in fear, and inspiration in desperation. They have a can-do attitude and carry a bundle of positivity with them wherever they go. They believe in a power larger than themselves. This belief helps them sustain passion amidst adversity and drive despite darkness.

These three attributes often travel together, but not everyone has all of them. They together help you adapt to stress, both externally and internally. External adaptation is maintaining optimal social and occupational functioning; internal adaptation is maintaining happiness and wellbeing. Both are required for a complete resilient response.

For some, the three attributes and such adaptations are innate; however, for most of us active effort is necessary. Two aspects of mindset help us with the effort—flexible thinking and humility.

Flexible Thinking and Humility

You can only scribble so much on a book that is already written and printed. For writing something new and fresh you need empty pages. Those come from flexible thinking and humility.

- Flexible thinking—Inner flexibility in thinking is a sign of health, while rigidity and getting stuck---not so much. Flexibility allows you to learn and grow. If you are confident, you already know everything that has to be known. Therefore, there is no hope for knowing. Flexibility doesn't mean not having an opinion; it means considering thoughts as hypothesis and actions as experiments. Flexible thinking assumes that the world around you will change, anticipates that change, and is proactive about how to respond to change.[118]

- Humility—Humility isn't feeling small or having low self-esteem. Humility is having an accurate self-worth and having a healthy self-esteem. It is the humble that are able to respectfully assert themselves when needed and accommodate to others' preferences when appropriate. They don't pick ego fights, they respect and value others' preferences, and they do not spend their day trying to defend themselves. Their healthy self-worth helps them be comfortable with being vulnerable, which allows them to take greater risks. They may look like soft cotton from the outside but are actually steel from the inside. Researchers often call this quality hardiness.

Hardiness

Very early in the evolution of our understanding of resilience in adults, researchers introduced the term hardiness. Research showed hardiness was associated with lower psychological distress and higher quality of life,[119,120] among other positive outcomes.[121-125] Hardiness has three elements—Challenge, control and commitment.[120]

- Challenge: Hardy people look at life's struggles as opportunities for growth rather than overwhelming obstacles. They roll with the punches. They believe that a fulfilling life is one where challenges are met head on; success and failure are of lesser consequence. They believe in engaging rather than withdrawing. With repeated engagement they find improvised innovative solutions even in hopeless situations. They are able to think inside and outside the box and also without the box. They aren't fearless but are able and willing to face up to their fear—a hallmark of courage.[126] Such attitude does wonders to their stress and wellbeing. For example, in a study on soldiers caught in an avalanche, task focused coping (I make plan of action) or emotion focused coping (I let my feelings out) was associated with lower PTSD compared to avoidant coping (I refuse to believe that it happened).[127] Similarly, among fire fighters, higher number of exposures increased their confidence in their skills.[128]

- Control: Hardy people believe that with effort, events can be changed. They focus on what they can control and let go of the rest, so they can save energy for the important and worthwhile. Such belief helps them engage with the challenge without experiencing undue distress.[129,130] If an event has already happened, they focus on their response rather than lamenting the past. For example, in a study on women who were assaulted, positive distancing (you accept the next best thing to what you wanted) was helpful, while wishful thinking (you wished that you could change the way you felt) was associated with greater distress.[131] Including misfortune as one part of life's overall experience without taking it personal helps one tackle the misfortune with greater grit. Such belief engenders hope, that combined with faith, helped the brave 9/11 victims.[132,133] We all can learn from children with disabilities. Each day they show up at school without a thought about what they don't have. They make the most of what nature has still left intact and surprise us with their accomplishments. They are truly a model of resilience. I often hear from the school teachers that not uncommonly, children with special needs are more focused and happier than children with no limitations.

- Commitment: Hardy people have a phenomenal ability to find and create meaning. They have a great way of turning the littlest of daily activities into something meaningful. Importantly, their meaning is prosocial; they have a broad diameter of existence. They are willing to let go of their personal pleasure, prioritizing collective benefits. Further, they align their short-term actions with their long-term meaning. Such meaning can help even in the most extreme situations. For example, one study found that among victims of torture, political activists with greater commitment to a cause had greater resilience.[134] Many of our life's commitments converge to cultivating deeper relationships—with the world and with the self.

The Fabric of Relationships

You are always in a relationship—with the world, its people, and yourself. You draw energy from this relationship. When you are treated well, you feel stronger and more resilient. A large body of research proves this contention. For example, a lack of perceived social support is one of the most significant risk factors for PTSD.[135] Greater social support has been associated with lower psychological distress (and higher resilience) among a variety of groups ranging from firefighters,[128] to Vietnam veterans,[136] Kosovian refugees,[137] and burn victims.[138]

The opposite of social support, feeling lonely, wreaks havoc on our wellbeing. Our biological system is designed to start sounding alarm sirens when we feel socially isolated—because animals that are left alone generally don't do very well. Perceived loneliness is extremely stress provoking and has been associated with a variety of illnesses including heart disease, stroke, and even early death.

One important aspect here is that loneliness or social connection is a lot about perception. You can be alone in a room yet feel connected with many; or surrounded by a hundred people yet feel alone. Resilient people create a circle of connections, with which they bond in a common mission.[139] So while having a supportive group enhances resilience, the most resilient among us have the ability to forge connections and form such a group around them. The connectedness, collaboration, and caring that such integration brings gives rise to a higher order resilience—community resilience.[140]

You are probably aware of the "home team advantage" in sports. This is supported by research. Not only you are more likely to win in front of the home crowd, in one study, British players playing in front of the home crowd had higher testosterone levels.[141] Thus, the perception that you are being supported can change your biology. The more you feel connected with others by genuinely wanting their good, the more you will feel at home—both in personal and professional life. With deeper connections you will be able to leverage the home team advantage all day long, no matter where you are playing. Won't that be nice?

Just as beauty expresses itself in countless ways—from sunsets to peacocks to tigers to humans—resilience also expresses itself in countless ways, depending on your background, chosen vocation, where you live, and more. I believe everyone is resilient in his or her unique way. A better question than asking if someone is resilient is to ask, in what domain is he or she resilient?

11. How Are You Resilient?

Grapes come in over ten thousand varieties. Champagne, Concord, Cotton Candy, Moon Drops, Sultana—each grape has its own flavor and sweetness. I have tasted some sour ones, but never bitter or salty grapes. When ripe, all grapes are sweet, though differently sweet. Resilience is also like that. No one has zero resilience and no one has a hundred. We all are somewhere in between. Our resilience changes depending on our wellbeing, our thoughts, and how the world treats us. Further, each of us have a unique flavor of resilience—we all are differently resilient. Let's explore these two ideas.

Everyone is Differently Resilient

What makes you strong? Can you lift a hundred pounds or run a marathon? Are you skilled at public speaking, great at connecting with people, or able to sit for ten hours writing a software code? We all have our unique strengths.

Most animal species have unique gifts that help them thrive in the milieu they live in. Camels can go for months without water, ants can carry three times their body weight, emperor penguins can survive for four months without eating, planarian worms can regenerate their entire body from a small little fragment (they have been cut into over 200 pieces, with each piece regenerating the entire worm), Turritopsis (a jelly fish) can go back to polyp stage and be a child again once it reaches a certain age or gets sick or injured, and Tardigrades (also called the moss piglet), a 0.5 mm eight-legged creature can withstand cooling to -272 degrees Celsius, heating to 150 degrees Celsius, can go without food or water for 30+ years, and can even survive in the vacuum of space. None of the human illusionists and endurance artists can match any of these feats. Instead, humans have a gift not in the realm of other animals—our capacity for imagination and deep thinking.

We use our thinking abilities to negotiate our complex world. I have met countless people who have overcome struggles that I thought could have crushed me if I was facing them. I have no doubt that you have unique areas of resilience that are truly worth admiring. Likely, you also have areas of weakness too. Often, your success depends on how much the world values and is willing to reward your strengths. And the world's valuations keep changing.

Your singing or acting ability wouldn't have taken you too far a thousand years ago, but that is not so now. Instead, a few thousand years ago your ability to throw spears, a skill of minimal value presently, would have put you at the top of the tribe. Recognizing this ever-changing valuation, it is best not to judge or compare but honor everyone for his or her strengths, knowing we all are strong in our own unique way.

Keep in mind as you go through the day that every person in front of you has unique strengths that would be very impressive if you were fully aware of their special skill set. With this awareness, respect them for who they are.

Resilience Changes with Time

Meteorologists compile multiple pieces of information—distribution of air pressure, solar energy, elevation, proximity to large water body, and more—and input all this data into computer models that help them predict the future state of the atmosphere. This includes the overall trend as well as precise details such as the temperature, humidity, chances of rain or snow, and anything else that is of local value. If there is one thing you can predict about the weather with certainty is that it changes, from one day to the next.

Your resilience also changes similarly, depending on your company, current activities, thoughts, the success of your recent efforts, the state of the world, and more. On one day you could be feeling well, empowered, secure, and connected and inspired, but on the other you could feel unwell, unworthy, incapable, uninspired, lonely, and depressed. Sometimes contradictory feelings may co-occur. Fear and courage, hope and despair, optimism and pessimism, strength and weakness—they all may exist together and confuse you. You may not always find rational reason for your feelings.

You have a choice. You can choose to judge yourself and others or work with how you and they feel. While snow in May isn't welcome, it isn't in your or my control. It might be best to flow with the way you and others feel, assuming that everyone is trying to do their best. If someone close is sensitive, assume they are having a bad day; if they are pushy assume they are wanting to feel important. This perspective has helped me avoid conflicts, maintain good relationships, and get the best out of people, all the while remaining focused on my most important job for that day.

Resilience assumes, anticipates, and is prepared for change. Because change is the nature of the world, this assumption and anticipation will allow you to flow with life rather than block it or be blocked by it. To me that is wisdom.

A step toward understanding others' strengths is to take a tally of your own strengths and weaknesses. Let's end this section with a moment of introspection.

How Are You Resilient?

Your response to the following five items will help you understand your strengths and weakness. Answer them to the best of your ability.

#1. Challenges you love to take:

_____

_____

#2. Challenges you can take but would rather avoid:

_____

_____

#3. Challenges you dread:

_____

_____

#4. Your phobias:

_____

_____

#5. Attractions you find irresistible:

_____

_____

Meditate on your responses to the individual items. The first one will give you an idea of your strengths. It may be physical capacity, public speaking, marketing, design, or something else for you. The second will suggest your personal preferences. If learning/doing some of these things makes you more successful and helps you fulfill your job, then it will be worthwhile to invest the time. What you wrote for the third and fourth items are situations you would probably want to bypass on most days.

The fifth one is important. I have seen some of the most brilliant people do indecent, immoral and stupid things because of lack of self-control. The attractions you find irresistible are best avoided. For example, if you had quit smoking twelve years ago and wish to remain abstinent, it will be best to avoid parties where tobacco is in the air and the company of people whose clothes smell of tobacco. Also have compassion for those who can't quit because it is indeed a difficult addiction to give up.

When you are assessing your strengths and weaknesses, do not compare yours with others. We are seldom very rational in our comparisons. From being grandiose to feeling unworthy, we have a way of making unhelpful comparisons. Often, we tend to compare our weaknesses with others' strengths and vice versa. That's a faulty comparison. You can't judge a hippopotamus's strength by its ability to fly. Honor yours and others' strengths and weaknesses. I once heard someone say, "Thank God for my spouse's imperfections. But for those, they would be married to someone else!

II

Why be Resilient?

12. Four Reasons

Some things are a no brainer. To me, resilience is one of them. Perhaps after reading the first eleven chapters, you feel the same way. Yet I hear well-meaning experts arguing against investing time and money in personal resilience. Here is their logic. "When we ask people to be more resilient, we are shifting the blame on them. The problem is with the system not the people. Let's first fix the system."

This message, with its populist tone, resonates with many. It is also partially true. The system indeed needs to be fixed. But here are some limitations of this argument:

1. Work isn't the only issue—An average citizen today carries enormous cognitive and emotional load. This load includes issues around money, work, health, relationships, crime, loneliness, politics, and more. We are also the most fearful we have ever been, with 74 percent of us fearful of corrupt government officials, our top current fear.[142] Urbanization and air pollution are increasing our stress.[143] Social media is raising our stress hormones (cortisol).[144] Researchers who suggest we don't need individual resilience will likely find themselves behind the curve when they notice that fixing the work-related issues (if that ever happens), doesn't fix the stress/burnout problem.

2. The system will never be completely fixed—I have never seen a solution that doesn't generate its own set of problems. Resources are finite while the need is almost always more than the available resources. The systems have become much more complex now; most problems aren't simple as a pebble in the shoe that can be removed to ease the pain. Finally, many problems need legislative and political will that isn't in the control of an individual or a single institution.

3. The 'They' mentality takes away locus of control—The moment you start hearing in a meeting, 'they want this' or 'they are doing this,' it is time to take a pause. When we start pointing at others for our problems, we shift locus of control. We give control to others and assume the place of the victim. We embrace the pediatric model of resilience since children are highly dependent on the outside world for their wellbeing. Even when we recognize that the system is at fault, keeping the locus of control within ourselves, looking at problems as worthy challenges, and becoming an inspired change agent, will be the path to find credible solutions.

4. Resilience is about empowering, not blaming—When was the last time you heard that a burnt out professional transformed the system? Marie Curie, Mahatma Gandhi, Helen Keller—they all worked under tremendous constraints. None of them had easier lives than us. The goal of resilience is to preserve the strength so you become the change agent instead of being passive bearers of change. Resiliency truly isn't about putting the onus on the individual. It is about preserving the individual. When treating a patient with bad pneumonia, we don't wait for the antibiotics to start working if the patient has low oxygen and is dehydrated. We give oxygen and fluids concurrently. Similarly, individual and organizational approaches have to happen concurrently. What good will be fixing the

system if by the time the system is fixed, all its members have left and the ones remaining are burnt out?

Three additional arguments support this case for resilience.

#1: The Opposite of Resilience is Status Quo or Worse

Three outcomes: In August of 1883, the prairies of Minnesota were hit by a series of tornadoes. One of them was a category F5 tornado, where the wind achieves an incredible speed of 261-318 mph. That tornado took 37 lives, injured over a hundred, and left a small town of 5100 people ravaged. A British surgeon who had emigrated to the U.S. in 1845 and lived in this town as its county doctor, along with his two sons took care of the victims, working round the clock for days. Lacking a local hospital, they converted a dance hall into a temporary emergency room.

Looking at their dedication, skills and work ethic, and perceiving local need, the sisters of Saint Francis proposed to the doctor that they will help build a clinic if he would staff it. He agreed. That small town was Rochester, Minnesota and the clinic grew to become one of the finest hospitals in the world, Mayo Clinic, that now cares for about 1.5 million patients every year.

The tornado was decidedly a tragedy at the time. But fast forward to today, its winds now spin hope, health, and healing for countless millions, not to mention thousands of new inventions and a Nobel prize. This is a classic resilient response—growing and transforming <u>because</u> of adversity.

The three outcomes of a disruption are:
- Remain disrupted
- Get back to status quo
- Grow higher than ever before because you got disrupted

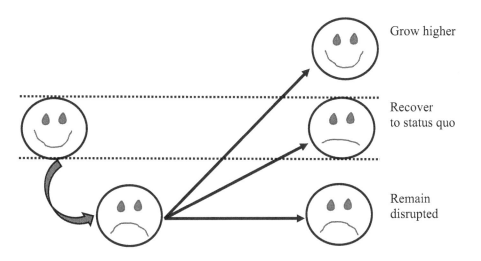

Grow higher

Recover
to status quo

Remain
disrupted

Unless we intentionally choose growth and put energy behind it, the default option would be to either remain disrupted or at best get back to status quo. This is true not only for the big societal events but also for everyday relationships, health challenges, and more.

Early on in our marriage, Richa and I disagreed on almost everything—which sofa to buy, what places to go, even which route to take for work. The outcome of most such disagreements was arguments that would linger in our ego shell for hours or days. Recovery was slow, hesitant and depended as much on chance as on intentional efforts. This lasted for several years with no promise of spontaneous improvement.

Gradually, we both realized there was a better way. We learned that the same thing can be accomplished in multiple different ways. Two educated people can have different opinions and preferences and that's okay. Just because someone isn't doing things your way, doesn't make him or her a bad person. People who disagree can still respect and love each other. We learned to accept, respect and love each other, disagreements and all.

The result—now every time we have an argument, we get to know a little more about each other. Our disagreements help us learn different ways of doing the same thing. That has helped us grow together. All of this was hard work initially. Over the years, however, intentional kindness has progressed to instinctive kindness, not only for each other but for the world at large. Our effort to respect and love each other has changed how we look at the world. I truly believe that if we had never argued, we would have never improved.

Growing because of adversity isn't optional. It is essential. Why? Because disruptions will happen again. Why go through the dishwasher twice when you can get cleaned up in the first wash? Growth also helps with one more resilience characteristic—the speed of recovery.

Faster the Better

At some point many of us realize that all our fears won't come true; we have greater strength than we thought; many of the annoying experiences actually help us in the long run; most people are struggling in their own unique way; compassion and forgiveness to ourselves is just as important as it is to others; and the best way to help ourselves is to get busy helping others. Once we internalize these realities, we start seeing life differently and become better at handling adversities. Time is an important factor here from two perspectives.

First, the sooner you gain this wisdom (i.e. earlier in life), the more years you get to live with a calmer head. I often compare this with going to a theme park. The earlier you show up, the more rides you get to enjoy.

Second, in a difficult experience the earlier you launch this wiser thinking, the quicker your recovery. Let's say you are driving. Someone cuts you off on the road. A number of negative responses are possible. If, however, you give others the benefit of doubt and assume that this person is perhaps rushing to the ER with a sick child, then you'll remain a safe driver and save your heart and brain from your own adrenaline attack. Similarly, in an argument, if very early on you remember that this person who is upset is actually hurting, the two of you will reach a much better place.

That wiser perspective won't happen automatically. It takes effort, practice and time. So be flexible about the timing of resilience. Depending on the type of trauma, some may recover fast and some may take more time.[145]

The brain has to use its "kindness circuit" thousands of times for that circuit to become the expressway. Hence the need to start training yourself the day you wake up to the need for change. Postponing by a week will likely result in postponing by a decade.

#2: Increasing Your Capacity to Lift the Load is the Low-hanging Fruit

Two solutions: If you have to move two-hundred pounds from one place to another and you can only lift ten pounds at a time, you can do two things to make it easier: one, lift only ten pounds at a time, and two, train your muscles so you can lift greater weight. The former optimizes the load (albeit at the cost of lower speed); and the latter increases your capacity to lift the load.

Optimizing the load is a great idea. You can delegate the work that isn't most meaningful for you. You can prioritize and pack your day with only the most important stuff. You can take a course in time (or priority) management. You can find ways of simplifying the work schedule. You can decrease your load by cutting your responsibilities and increasing your team size. And even more.

Problem-specific solutions are desirable whenever feasible. These solutions, thoughtfully planned and implemented, definitely help. If there is a thorn stuck in your finger, then taking out the thorn is the obvious solution. You don't have to sit there and philosophize about the need for thorns in the universe. However, most of our problems are much more complex.

In a corporate environment, decreasing the load and hiring more people has another problem—it will impact profitability. When was the last time your request for hiring more people to do the same job was met with great warmth?

The other challenge is that a significant proportion of the load is emotional. As we develop more connections and get older, a greater emotional load accumulates. The emotional load feeds into itself and is difficult, if not nearly impossible to delegate.

Increasing your capacity to lift the load by building resilience is the second approach. Until very recently, this approach wasn't accessible to us. That was because we had little idea about how our ultimate experiencer, our brain, operates. Thus, our solutions weren't informed by research. A lot has changed in the past few decades. The gist of it is that cutting edge scientific insights now have uncovered how we can make ourselves more resilient by training and strengthening specific areas of the brain. In fact, developing, testing, and disseminating such solutions is my life's work.[146]

My team's research has shown that you can learn the requisite skills in as little as two hours, and you need only five to ten minutes during the day to practice them. The resulting resilience building can have widespread positive effects on different aspects of one's being—physical, cognitive, emotional, spiritual, social, and occupational. Indeed, we have found in our research that increasing resilience improves not only stress, anxiety, quality of life, happiness, mindfulness, but also health behaviors, self-reported productivity, and has a trend towards decreasing number of sick days.[147] The overall cost in both time and resources is minimal, and the benefits far reaching. I have no doubt in the coming decades such approaches will be more broadly implemented.

Going back to our argumentative phase of life—my wife and I could have tried to do precisely what the other person wanted. However, we would have failed in that effort. That isn't desirable either. The second choice, to better understand the other person, become wiser, more patient, kind and accepting, seems much more realistic. It offers a long-term sustainable solution, helping us improve our relationship with each other through becoming a better person while preserving our identity.

#3: Research Supports the Benefits of Resilience

Three strikes in a sequence result in a stress-related mental disorder (the three-hit concept).[97] The first hit is a vulnerable genotype (for example, the short form of 5HTTLPR). The second hit is an adverse early-life environment. A combination of these two predispose to the third hit—an adverse late-life environment.

The individual differences in reaction to an unpleasant situation, ranging from spilled milk to spouse philandering, strongly depends on their neurochemistry and the design of their brain networks orchestrated by their genes conditioned by the quality of upbringing. The sum total effect of the three hits can be captured in individual level of resilience.

In the next four chapters, I share with you research evidence that supports the argument that resilience has positive effect on psychological, physical, occupational, and social aspects of life. Let's dive deeper into research at this point.

13. Resilience and Physical Health (Part 1)

Thoughts are subtle invisible products of the brain's activity. Like waves on a beach, they incessantly appear one after the other, with the next thought wiping the impressions left by the previous one. When thoughts band together and take control over our being by taking charge of our brain, they wield enormous power. Their strength also originates from an important natural phenomenon, the power of the subtle over the gross.

Subtle is Powerful

Often when I look at an eighteen-wheeler I think about the fuel that powers it—a thin liquid that evaporates when exposed to the air. If you didn't know the physics of an internal combustion engine, it will be nearly impossible to imagine that a gallon of this thin liquid (gasoline) has the energy to move the massive forty tons by six miles. It'll be even more difficult to imagine how liquid hydrogen powers one of the strongest vehicles man has ever created—the space shuttle.

I share this to emphasize the power of the subtle. While a thick wall of steel looks more domineering than a beam of light, when this beam gets organized into very narrow wavelength as laser it splits the steel. The earth's magnetic field, an invisible unfelt force, prevents the atmosphere from evaporating while dueling against the solar flares that hit us. Mars lost its atmosphere and turned into a cold and arid world when it lost its magnetic field. Many subtle, thin, invisible, and barely felt entities are much more powerful than others that look and feel solid, heavy, impenetrable, and hard.

What is even more subtle than any of the above-mentioned forces? I believe subtler and more powerful than any of the forces I mentioned above is the stream generated by your brain's activity—your thoughts.

Thoughts are a product of the systematic firing of a group of neurons. I look at thoughts as switches. They turn on or off specific parts of the brain's machinery, with a downstream effect on the entire body. The part of the brain that is turned on depends on the particular thought. With respect to their short-term impact, thoughts are of two kinds.

Random disorganized thoughts are like the waves on a lake. They appear and dissolve without much consequence. But every so often the second form of thought emerges, one that is focused, organized, and powerful—much like a tall wave, sometimes a tsunami. Such a thought, particularly if it has a negative flavor, can turn on the brain's fear/stress machinery. What follows is a chain reaction of expanding destruction. Let's look at some of the pathways/mechanisms that are involved in this reaction.

Early Responders

The purpose of the stress response is to focus the brain's attention on the threat and direct the body's energies for the immediate fight. Non-essential functions (that can be postponed) like immune regulation, reproduction, and digestion are deferred. The body is also preparing for healing the wounds and blood loss—thus increasing inflammation and promoting clotting factors in the blood.[148] You can see how a well-meaning response, when protracted, can hurt us in the long-term. Here is how it works:

Stressful thought or a threatening sight or sound alerts the brain to prepare itself for the impending fight or flight. The first responder is the amygdala, an almond shaped nucleus at the base of the brain, that, not unlike the sensors of a security system, sniffs every input for threat. The moment it senses danger, the amygdala reprioritizes the brain's activity. It shuts down all dispensable brain operations and focuses your brain on the immediate threat.

An early step in this process is recruitment of the locus coeruleus (LC), a tiny area (only made of about 50,000 neurons compared to the 86 billion in the brain) that is packed with noradrenaline (the brain version of adrenaline). Like the amygdala, LC is very powerful for two reasons. One, it is extremely well networked. Almost every lieutenant of the brain receives input from LC. Second, despite its diminutive size, LC is the single largest source of noradrenaline in our brain. Why is this a big deal? It is because noradrenaline is involved in critical roles such as attention, arousal, memory, and the stress response. Your powerful cerebral cortex (that hosts all your higher mental functions) depends on LC as its sole supplier of noradrenaline.

The hypothalamus is another early responder in the stress response. It is the portal of entry for the endocrine glands. Through its connection with the pituitary gland, the hypothalamus facilitates release of various stress hormones. It also helps with arousal, learning, sleep-wake cycle, temperature regulation, and several other body functions.

These early responders activate extremely quickly, even before you have fully comprehended the nature and extent of the threat. They wake up your body and turn on two systems to mobilize energy, focus your attention, regulate your memory and stop any distracting activity. Let's look at them next.

The Body is Awakened

The two systems that now take charge are the SAM and the HPA. SAM is the sympathetic-adrenal-medullary system. It activates fast, like 911. Its primary arsenal is adrenaline and related hormones. They lock on the receptors of many different organs— heart, lungs, liver, muscles, endocrine glands, and immune system—to immediately start the stress/survival response.

HPA is the hypothalamic-pituitary-adrenocortical axis. This system is a multi-step process. Its primary arsenal is the corticosteroids and other related hormones. After a little delay, they take the baton from adrenaline and continue its good work to focus your body and brain on survival.

The above two are the core mediators that are crucial to your survival in the short-term. This system, however, wasn't designed to remain active for days, weeks, and months, which is how it is often deployed in the modern times.

Sacrificing the Long Term

Our stress machinery prioritizes the short term while sacrificing the long term. A number of changes mediate this shift in priority. SAM and HPA keep churning adrenaline and steroids. The vagus nerve, which is a key effector of the parasympathetic system that helps us rest and digest, becomes less active.[149] Critical areas of the brain that help you remember, focus and make rational decisions (the hippocampus and the prefrontal cortex) atrophy with ongoing stress.[150,151] The brain, as a result, shifts from well thought out goal-directed responses to habitual simpler instinctive reactions.[152,153]

Simultaneously, your immune system becomes less effective in fighting external and internal bugs.[154-156] Coupled with the weakened immune system, the chemicals that host inflammation increase; your inflammatory pathways thus become more active.[157,158] Further, your blood thickens with increase in clotting factors and platelets become stickier.[159,160] The inner lining of your blood vessels (endothelium) becomes less healthy.[161] You care less about yourself[162] and might gain weight from dysregulated eating.[163] These changes predispose to recurrent infections, inflammatory disorders (that range from lupus to cancer),[164] weakened bones and muscles, autoimmune disorders,[165] elevated blood sugars, blocked blood vessels (resulting in heart attack and stroke),[166] serious abnormal heart rhythms,[167] and more.[168,169]

At a cellular level, chronic stress shortens telomeres, increases expression of pro-inflammatory genes, causes abnormalities in protein folding—changes that might underlie the more obvious findings like elevated inflammatory markers, immune suppression, and clotting. These changes also predispose to Alzheimer's disease, Parkinson's disease and other neurodegenerative disorders,[170-172] as well as accelerated aging.[173]

Recognize that our stress response was developed when external injuries were the number one cause of death. We died young. This system wasn't tested for the long term. Going back even a few hundred years, medical autopsies seldom reported coronary blockages as the cause of death. But now we die mostly from heart disease, stroke, cancer, unchecked inflammation, infections—conditions worsened by the stress response.

There is one more aspect that hurts us—our response is agnostic to the type of stressor, and whether it is real or not.

Emotional=Physical; Imaginary=Real

Recall the first time you got up to speak in front of the class. How much of a surge in adrenaline did you experience? Perhaps it was no different compared to the surge you might experience if you are being chased by a wild dog. If you have spider phobia, an ominous-looking spider in the basement might cause the same adrenaline release as an armed intruder. Mentally escaping a yelling supervisor can generate more cortisol than escaping a grizzly bear.

While our stressors have changed, our stress machinery is still playing catch up. We have a single generic stress response. No matter the type of threat, the same players come into action. These players do not have a free will. They are just following the commands. They are charged with protecting us, both our physical and emotional body. An emotional hurt injures our physical heart the same way as the threat of a physical hurt. That is the hallmark of stress-heart syndrome, a known medical condition.

It doesn't stop here. Brain responders can't parse between imaginary and real. Thus, the thought of a snake can be as scary as watching one. This is because for a species that has such wonderful ability to imagine, imaginary is real. We have used this skill to create our beautiful world but also to make ourselves miserable.

In its efforts to keep it simple, nature has gifted us a stress response that overshoots and misfires way more than it needs to. Sending fire trucks every time someone lights a matchstick or a sparkler downtown won't be a good idea. That's precisely what our stress response does. Many wars originate in paranoia and false fears. Such wars can hurt millions and cost trillions.

At an individual level, unchecked stress creates a state of war in our being. It clogs our arteries, hollows our brain, creates inflammation, causes unchecked infections, predisposes to cancer, hampers creativity and productivity, hurts relationships and takes away joy from life. Pick up the index of any medical book. Every single diagnosis is made worse by excessive stress.[174-180]

Like a few weeds that appear in your yard, if unchecked they can multiply and eventually take over the entire yard, unchecked stress may seem innocuous in the short term, but is extremely harmful in the long term.

So much for stating the problem! Let's now take a look at some promising results from resilience research.

14. Resilience and Physical Health (Part 2)

We just learned how thoughts can act as switches to recruit the powerful stress machinery. This machinery once launched whips our hearts and muscles into overdrive and squeezes our glands to release potent chemicals, adversely affecting every system of our body.[181] These chemicals are helpful in the short term but toxic and damaging in the long term.[182]

Resilience can help in multiple ways. First, resilience changes the sensitivity of the switch, so the machinery launches only when something big and substantial, worth-reacting happens. Second, resilience can help you regulate the strength of the response, so your stress response is proportionate to the short-term need. Third, resilience can help you douse the response as soon as it stops serving an adaptive purpose. Having a sense of control, optimism, pragmatic acceptance, self-esteem, and spirituality all helps. Fourth, resilience helps with adherence to treatment, self-care, perception of illness and investment of time and effort in wellbeing.[183] Finally, resilience can help you build reserves so your organs individually, and your body as a whole, is better able to withstand the damage caused by excessive stress.

What follows in this chapter is some of the research evidence from individual studies about the benefits of resilience in helping your physical health. Here is the gist of the research—*Psychological resilience fosters physical resilience, both in health and disease.* If you are already convinced of this and/or are likely to find the details of the research studies boring, then you are welcome to skim through the information and come back to it at a later time.

Cancer

The best research information is available for patients with cancer. Several dozen studies have shown that higher resilience (and the ingredients that contribute to resilience) correlate with better physical outcomes among patients with cancer. Summarized below are a few of the studies.

- Higher self-efficacy and social support predicted resilience to decline among 594 older cancer survivors.[24]

- In 1823 hematopoietic cell transplantation patients, lower resilience was associated with lower performance, higher severity of chronic graft versus host disease, missing work, and permanent disability. Low resilience also correlated with higher psychological distress and lower mental health related quality of life.[184]

- In 75 patients undergoing allogeneic stem cell transplantation, resilience positively correlated with quality of life and social functioning, and negatively correlated with anxiety and depression. The more resilient individuals also had higher physical, emotional, and social functioning, and greater self-efficacy.[185]

- In 239 patients with cancer treated with radiotherapy, higher resilience correlated with lower fatigue early in treatment.[186]

- In 1588 patients with breast cancer, lower psychological distress predicted longer recurrence free and overall survival.[187]

- In a study involving 460 patients with breast cancer, both chronic and episodic stress was associated with higher risk of bothersome physical symptoms, during and after treatment.[188]

- Exceptional cancer survivors had higher resilience, and psychological variables explained considerable variance in well-being.[189]

- In a review of 11 studies in patients with cancer, resilience was associated with better psychological wellbeing, mental, and physical health.[190]

- In a study of 343 patients with cancer, higher resilience was associated with greater physical activity and lower psychological distress.[191]

Other Medical Conditions

Resilience has been studied in several other medical conditions. Here are some of them.

- **Cardiovascular:** High trait resilience was associated with greater heart rate and blood pressure recovery from stress anticipation exposures compared to low trait resilience. High trait resilience also showed greater systolic and diastolic blood pressure habituation across two successive stress anticipation exposures.[192] In patients with pre-existing heart disease, high stress was associated with worse outcomes, including increased risk of death.[193]

- **Asthma:** In 677 Aboriginal youth, higher resilience was associated with significantly lower self-reported asthma symptoms and caregiver reported lifetime health problems.[194]

- **Kidney disease:** Resilience correlated with better self-care in patients with end-stage kidney disease.[195]

- **Parkinson's disease:** High stress has been associated with increased risk of Parkinson's disease.[170] In 83 patients with Parkinson's disease, greater resilience was associated with lower disability, and better physical and mental health. The more resilient patients also had less fatigue, less apathy, less depression, and more optimism.[196]

- **Diabetes:** Stress increases risk of diabetes,[197] and in patients with diabetes, resilience resources predicted future HbA1c and buffered worsening HbA1c and self-care behaviors in the face of rising distress levels.[198] In a study of 140 patients with diabetes, a close corollary of resilience—optimism, was found to be associated with lower stress reactivity and lower cortisol output.[199] In a meta-analysis that looked at resiliency training in patients with diabetes and hypertension, some correlation was noticed with improvement in average blood glucose levels.[200] In 242 patients with diabetes, resilience was associated with better physical and psychological functioning.[201]

- **Addictions:** In a study involving 1249 urban residents, resilience moderated the relationship between anxiety and depression, and tobacco use.[202] In a non-controlled before-after intervention among 1449 grade 7-10 students, resilience intervention decreased tobacco, alcohol, and marijuana use.[203]

- **Chronic pain:** Research shows resilience has significant impact on pain perception and could help with better pain control.[204]

- **Traumatic brain injury:** Resilience was a predictor of lower self-reported fatigue among 67 patients with mild traumatic brain injury, even after adjusting for insomnia, pain and depressive symptoms.[205]

- **Memory:** Acute, recent and chronic stress—all negatively affect memory,[206] increase accumulation of amyloid in the brain, predispose to inflammation, and thus increase the risk of dementia.[207]

Overall Health

- In children, in a meta-analysis of 14 studies with 12,772 participants, protective factors for stress had a moderate effect and vulnerability factors had small-moderate negative effect on physiological measures, sleep behavior, and overall health.[208]

- Lower levels of wellbeing was associated with lower level of resilience among 194 chiropractic students.[209]

- In 1350 medical students, compared to students with very high resilience levels, students with very low resilience levels had lower quality of life, lower perception of educational environment, and worse physical health.[210]

- In a study involving 185 American Indians, resilience was associated with higher physical and mental health and lower pain.[211]

- In a study involving war veterans, resilience was associated with better mental health and physical health outcomes.[212]

Aging

- In a study involving 10,753 participants between 51-98 years of age, higher resiliency protected against activities of daily living (ADL) and instrumental activities of daily living (IADL) limitations related to aging and chronic illness over a two-year period.[213]

- Higher self-efficacy and social support predicted resilience to decline among 594 older patients.[214]

- In another study, resilience mediated the effect of perceived stress on physical health functioning and self-rated successful aging among 1006 older adults.[215]

Interesting, isn't it, how psychological resilience leads to better physical health. What amazes me is that this is such a low-hanging fruit to help us get stronger and healthier, yet the vast majority of us aren't even aware of the construct.

The benefits of resilience aren't limited to just physical wellbeing. A large body of research shows that building resilience is a very effective way to improve happiness, relationships, and mental health. Let's turn to that next.

15. Resilience and Psychological Wellbeing

We are wealthier than any previous generation. We also have access to some phenomenal gadgets. But somehow, all our technological and financial success isn't adding up to widespread happiness. If anything, it is the other way around. Loneliness is an epidemic. Trust is at a record low, and stress and fear at a record high. Our choices are guided less by seeking higher meaning and more by avoiding fear—the equivalent of driving with air bags already deployed.

Compared to our ancestors, we have swapped acute severe occasional stress for chronic moderate constant stress. We have also increased sensory pleasures from accumulating more 'stuff', while losing emotional pleasures from deep nurturing relationships. I can't think of a time when resilience would be more needed.

The good news is that a large body of literature shows us that for a variety of stressors among patients, students, and healthy adults, resilience is associated with lower stress and better mental health.

Patients

- Resilience was associated with lower psychological distress in renal transplant recipients.[216]

- Higher level of resilience positively impacted response to pharmacotherapy with or without therapy in 95 patients with mood disorders.[217]

- Among 51 patients undergoing hematopoietic stem cell transplant and their 45 relatives, higher resilience was associated with lower level of psychiatric symptoms.[218]

- In 40 children with cancer, resilience mediated the relationship between cancer symptom distress and quality of life.[219]

- In 51 caregivers of patients with head and neck cancer, higher resilience was associated with lower depression and anxiety. Stage of the primary cancer was not.[220]

- Resilience helped with psychosocial adjustment in 200 patients with digestive system cancer.[43]

- In 95 participants who had experienced trauma, three virtues (i.e., conscientiousness, vitality, and relationship) and resilience both correlated positively with post-traumatic growth and negatively with post-traumatic stress disorder (PTSD) symptoms.[52]

- Resilience directly influenced psychological distress in patients with GI cancer. In this study, resilience did not directly affect quality of life, fatigue, or treatment side effects.[221]

- In 91 couples coping with cancer, resilience of both partners negatively correlated with their psychological distress.[222]

- In patients with colorectal cancer, resilience mediated the effects of age and gender on emotional distress.[223]

- In 152 patients with cancer, psychological resilience was associated with lower levels of emotional distress. Patients with the highest resilience had 90 percent lower emotional distress compared to patients with lowest resilience.[224]

- In patients with ultra-high risk for schizophrenia, during the prodromal phase, low resilience was associated with higher risk of conversion to frank psychosis.[225]

- Resilience was associated with lower psychological distress in patients with spinal cord injury.[226]

Students

- In a study of 359 students who were exposed to campus shooting at Seattle Pacific University, resilience prevented development of post-traumatic stress, while gratitude fostered post-traumatic growth.[45]

- In a study involving 560 medical and psychology students at University of Adelaide, higher resilience was associated with lower psychological distress.[227]

- Positive emotions and resilience among 200 postdoctoral research fellows decreased the effect of stress on symptoms of anxiety and depression.[53]

- In a study involving 2925 Chinese medical students, higher resilience correlated with higher life satisfaction. The positive effect of higher resilience was more than the protective effect of lower stress.[228]

- In a randomized clinical trial involving 64 college students, resilience intervention was associated with significant total growth comprising of self-esteem, self-leadership, hopeful coping, and depressive symptoms.[229]

- In 202 vocation school nursing students, higher psychological resilience was associated with post-traumatic growth.[230]

- In a study involving 513 dietitians, nurses, physicians, social workers, clinical trainees, and health researchers, participants showed significant improvement in stress, mindfulness, empathy, and resilience with elective mind-body training.[231]

- Resilience correlated with better psychological wellbeing and engagement-related coping among 208 nursing professionals from University Hospital of Fuenlabrada (Madrid).[232]

- In a study involving 155 medical students, lower resilience and negative coping were associated with greater stress.[233]

- In college students, resilience was negatively associated with neuroticism, and positively related to extraversion and conscientiousness. Further, resilience moderated the relationship between emotional neglect and current psychiatric symptoms.[234]

Healthy Adults

- In a sample of 305 middle aged adults, resilience positively predicted psychological wellbeing, while emotional coping (avoidance) negatively predicted psychological wellbeing.[54]

- In 184 women with unsuccessful IVF, higher resilience correlates with lower symptoms of depression.[48]

- Resilience was a significant negative predictor of psychological distress among 75 refugees.[235]

- Among 199 infertile couples, high resilience was associated with better quality of life.[236]

- In 272 veterans, resilience meditated the effect of low unit support on depression.[237]

- Among 351 tennis players, greater mental toughness and greater resilience was correlated, and both were associated with lower stress level.[238]

- Resilience was associated with more task-oriented coping among 235 Spanish athletes.[239]

- In a review of 13 studies, resilience training was associated with improvement in several resilience and wellbeing measures.[240]

If you have a pill that decreases your chance of falling sick, helps you recover faster, helps you be happier, and empowers you to better handle your stress, it is very likely that you will take a 90-day supply with three refills. That pill is resilience. Further, it also improves two very important aspects of your life—your relationships and your work.

16. Resilience and Work

That was a tough day, our younger daughter's second birthday. We celebrated it with much fanfare. She was running a low-grade fever and had an upset stomach. Busy with making sure everyone ate the appetizers and cake and took the return gifts, we neglected giving her our full attention. She got dehydrated. By the time we decided to act, she was already drowsy, tired, and had dry skin. We felt tremendously guilty.

In the ER, we needed to access a vein to give her IV fluids. Her veins were all but collapsed. The first nurse arrived to insert the IV. She looked caring but unsure and defensive. I didn't have a good feeling about it. She certainly tested our patience with three pokes and no success. She finally gave up, promising to come back with someone more experienced. Someone more resilient, I hoped.

The next nurse walked in. She had an air of comfort, kindness, engagement, and presence that was immediately reassuring. She explained what she would do. I had no doubt she would find the vein. With utmost patience, she took ten minutes to find the right vein, prepped the skin and in one go, she was in. We were relieved. With the fluid replenished, our daughter perked up in no time. Life was good again.

The second nurse clearly had a different presence. She made us feel like we were in good hands. She was comfortable in her skin. She didn't think about failure. She seemed in control. She was caring but didn't struggle with emotions. Her confidence was palpable. It was clear she had dealt with similar or tougher situations before. I would capture all her wonderful skills in one word—resilient.

Personally, I don't need research studies to prove to me that resilience can enhance performance at work. I have worked with enough colleagues, supervisors, and mentees who would buckle under the least pressure and operated from a place of fear. I have also worked with people who I know will give their best and can be fully trusted with responsibility. Having said that, it will still help to look at some of the studies.

Resilience and Work

- Resilience was associated with less distraction or disengagement related coping among 235 Spanish athletes.[239]

- Resilience was associated with lower psychological distress and academic burnout among 113 nurses.[241]

- Resilience impacted the relationship between mindfulness, self-efficacy, and coping, and burnout scores among 422 nurses/students across Australia and Canada.[242]

- Practitioner effectiveness correlated with mindfulness and resilience in a survey of 37 practitioners.[243]

- In a small study using a program to enhance psychological capital, the training not only enhanced psychological capital, but also improved on-the-job performance.[244]

- In 605 undergraduate students, high intrapersonal resilience correlated with higher cumulative GPA, aptitude and achievement.[245]

- In 74 minority faculty members, higher resilience correlated with better educational and academic productivity.[246]

- In 13 studies among physicians, resilience was associated with higher persistence and self-directedness, and lower avoidance of challenges; resilience was associated with traits supporting high function levels in demanding professional roles.[247]

- In a study involving 40 depressed professionals, mindfulness-based resilience training was associated with significant reduction in depression, stress, anxiety and presenteeism.[248]

- In a study involving 947 restaurant workers in 28 restaurants, team resilience training was associated with a significant reduction in exposure to problem coworkers and personal stress.[249]

- In a clinical trial involving 44 high school teachers, a cognitive-behavior based program reduced stress, enhanced goal attainment, wellbeing, and resilience.[250]

- In a randomized study involving 133 female doctoral students, participants were offered an online program to enhance persistence in their career. The study showed improved problem solving, resilience, and coping efficacy. They also showed enhanced persistence.[251]

- In a study involving 53 lubricant sales managers, participation in an online resilience program was reported to be suboptimal without significant change in the tested outcomes.[252]

- In a study involving 2063 workers, resilience was found to be protective of burnout, sleep problems, likelihood of depression, job satisfaction, intent to quit, absences, and productivity.[253]

- In a study involving 18 police officers, the effect of a 10-week imagery and skills training program was tested compared to training as usual. The results showed less negative mood, less heart rate reactivity, and better police performance compared to controls.[254]

- In a randomized clinical trial involving 41 executives of a public health agency, participants received four coaching sessions and half-day leadership training, over 10 weeks. The program was associated with improved wellbeing and resilience, and lower depression and stress.[255]

- In a study assessing the performance of anesthesiologists, researchers found that nontechnical skills (such as leadership, social skills) were extremely important for technical performance, particularly in situations likely to create high levels of stress.[256]

- In a study involving 133 human service professionals, higher resilience and mindfulness was associated with lower levels of psychological distress and burnout.[257]

- In a review reporting on web-based approaches for work-related stress, 48 such programs were identified, mostly based on relaxation, mindfulness, and cognitive behavioral therapy.[258] However, the data on their effectiveness was sparse and not fully convincing.

Work-related stress has been shown to affect attention, judgment and decision making among employees.[259] Examination stress has been shown to decrease neuroplasticity in the brain, which can hamper learning.[260] It is thus heart-warming to see that in the last decade, several groups have emerged offering online and in-person resilience programs often based on cognitive behavioral therapy and mindfulness.[261-264] Not all of these programs presently have convincing efficacy data. The overall trend, however, is very positive, with increasing philanthropic, entrepreneurial, and scientific interests in developing this field. In addition to individual resilience, leadership, and a resilient culture contributing to organizational resilience, an additional advantage of work resilience and wellbeing programs is their positive impact on the corporate bottom line, both with respect to work performance and health care costs (average ROI of $2 to $3 for each dollar spent).[265-269]

In the last chapter of this book, I will briefly share some information about the Stress Management and Resilience Training (SMART) program we have developed and shared with over half a million people over the previous ten years. This program has a special emphasis on the very important part of your life—relationships.

17. Resilience and Relationships

The constructs of language, time, evolution, and culture all converge to their main ingredient—stories. I once heard someone say that the universe isn't made of atoms, it is made of stories. Our stories thrive in the fabric of our relationships.

At any moment, you are in three relationships—with others, with yourself, and with what you consider sacred. A fulfilled life integrates these three relationships in a cohesive, seamless, mutually enriching manner.

Writing the conclusions for the 75-year-long Grant study at Harvard, researchers summed up the core findings in these simple words, "Warmth of relationships throughout life has the greatest positive impact on life satisfaction."[270] Researchers also noted, "Happiness is love. Full stop." Further, the effect of positive relationships extended more broadly into life, particularly into work. For example, warm relationships among men with mothers was associated with increased yearly earnings by a whopping $87,000. A positive relationship was also associated with greater effectiveness at work.

It's All About Relationships

In a survey of 835 employees from public, private, and nonprofit firms in Britain, researchers asked the participants about the biggest drain on resilience at work.[271] The number one cause acknowledged by 75 percent of the workers was managing difficult relationships and politics at the workplace. The core source of resilience for 90 percent of the participants was a healthy relationship with the self, and for 50 percent, with others.

Our brain carries two loads—cognitive and emotional. The cognitive load is all the stuff we have to remember and do to run our life. While the cognitive load is overwhelming for many, it is the emotional load, the load of hurts, regrets, concerns, fears, sensitivities, unmet expectations, and more that is so much more difficult to lift. The main source of emotional load is relationships, hence their outsized importance in our wellbeing.

This is compounded by the many platforms we use to connect with each other. Very likely you have people in your life who you meet in person, on the phone, by text, email, through social media, and more. You may have noticed that people's personalities change depending on the platform. Some people are sweeter in person and cold and distant on the phone, text, or email. Others are just the opposite. So for each person we are connecting with five or more personalities. This makes our relationships even more complex.

None of this is helped by the insecurity in our relationships. Our moods are labile and dependent on countless influences that impact our self-worth, optimism, and satisfaction. It is thus very difficult for anyone to be completely secure in any relationship.

No wonder we find that our greatest source of joy as well as sorrow is our relationships, an aspect of life significantly affected by resilience.

Research with Relationships

In a study involving 1954 participants, my colleagues and I looked at the correlation of resilience with a number of aspects of relationships. Higher resilience correlated with:

- Higher support from friends and family
- Lower stress from household chores
- Lower stress from household finances
- Better quality of family life
- Better quality of current marriage
- Greater intimacy in relationship
- Greater fairness in sharing of responsibilities
- Higher number of friends
- Higher number of close friends

We will be publishing these findings in upcoming scientific publications.

Several additional studies have reported on the positive effect of resilience on relationships.

- Resilience mediated the relationship between parental divorce and children's mental health.[272]

- In parents of children with cancer, lower resilience was associated with higher distress, lower social support, and lower family function. They also had more sleep difficulties, lower health satisfaction, and decreased ability to express worries to the medical team.[273]

- In 2025 veterans, of those with high number of life traumas, 69.5 percent were resilient. Resilient participants had greater social connectedness (i.e., secure attachment style, social support) and lower physical health difficulties and psychiatric problems.[274]

- In a study involving 232 government employees, enhancing personal resilience was associated with improvement in interpersonal relationships.[275]

None of this should be surprising. If you started a practice that improves your physical health, lowers your stress, enhances your happiness, and helps you be more successful at work, it is very likely that it will start affecting how you relate with yourself and others, and thus all your relationships.[276] This sets you in a positive feedback loop because positive relationships by themselves enhance your physical health, happiness, success, and overall resilience. The figure below summarizes the connection between resilience, wellbeing, and relationships.

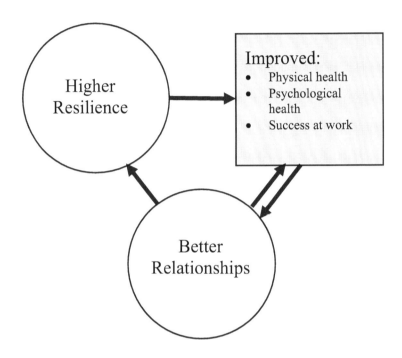

In the next and final chapter, I will summarize all the topics we have discussed in this book and also share a few suggestions on how best to enhance your resilience, a topic I have covered in several previous books and will be discussing in a future manuscript.

18. Summary

I hope the preceding two sections have provided you a good framework of what is resilience and why resilience is one of the most important attributes that can lift every aspect of your life. Here is a summary of the topics we have covered:

In chapter 1, we learned that resilience is best captured in a story and I invited you to think about someone in your personal life you consider very resilient. We also explored what makes this person resilient.

In chapter 2, we explored a few definitions of resilience and looked at resilience as a trait, a process, and an outcome. We also touched upon the intimate relationship between resilience and adversity.

In chapter 3, we discussed the origins of resilience in physical sciences from where it was adopted by ecology and psychology. We then tracked resilience research in children, mostly in relation to growing up in adverse environments, and then moved on to resilience in adults, in acute traumatic situations such as wars, and then in relation to chronic stressors.

In chapter 4, we separated resilience from stress management by considering stress management as focusing on the past and being reactive and recovery centric, while resilience is focusing on the future, and being proactive and growth centric.

In chapter 5, we learned from mangoes, bamboo, and willow trees, three core concepts about resilience—when exposed to heat, ripen don't burnout; bend so you do not break; and be flexible about preferences and strong about principles.

In chapter 6, we looked at the example of sickle cell anemia and malaria to understand how sometimes vulnerability can be a resilience factor.

In chapter 7, we looked at the four domains of resilience—physical, cognitive, emotional, and spiritual. Physical resilience is being strong, recovering fast, and having good reserve to withstand illness. Cognitive resilience is having good attention, memory, and judgment, and preserving these abilities when challenged. Emotional resilience is experiencing authentic positive emotions and recovering relatively quickly from negative emotions. Spiritual resilience is having a secure deeper meaning and not losing that meaning through the ups and downs of life.

In chapter 8, we got deeper into science and looked at how genes influence our resilience, and how resilience influences our genes through epigenetics.

In chapter 9, we investigated the brain chemistry and looked at the chemicals that accelerate and brake our stress response as well as the ones that have a dual influence.

In chapter 10, we explored the three aspects of the resilient mindset—other centricity, role models, and hopeful world construct. We also explored the concept of hardiness and its three ingredients—challenge, control, and meaning.

In chapter 11, we realized that resilience isn't a yes or no phenomenon. Instead, every person is resilient in his or her unique way. We also saw that resilience is a dynamic phenomenon and changes with the changing reality within and around us.

In chapter 12, we looked at four reasons why resilience is a good idea. They include the broad spectrum of challenges we face today in an increasingly complex world, the realization that the external world will always be offering unique challenges, the recognition that blaming the system and waiting for it to change is giving away control, and resilience is about empowering and modeling the strength embraced by many of our role models who chose the path of strength despite tremendous adversity and personal difficulties.

In chapter 13, we discussed the basics of the stress response, particularly how a negative thought can initiate a cascade of reactions which can wreak havoc on our physical body. Further, this cascade prioritizes short-term survival while short-changing long-term wellbeing.

In chapter 14, we explored the relationship between lower resilience and a number of physical conditions including cancer, cardiovascular disease, asthma, kidney disease, Parkinson's disease, diabetes, addictions, chronic pain, and traumatic brain injury. We also looked at the positive relationship between resilience and overall health and slowed aging.

In chapter 15, we evaluated the positive relationship between resilience and psychological wellbeing among patients, students, and healthy adults.

In chapter 16, we looked at how resilience can have a positive impact on our work.

In chapter 17, we evaluated the effect of resilience on the most important part of our life—our relationships.

Enhancing Resilience

An important question now is this—Is resilience fixed or can it be increased? The answer is a definite yes for the assertion that resilience can be increased. Next, I will provide a partial list of a number of activities/skills that can enhance your resilience.

- Healthy diet
- Exercise
- Restorative sleep
- Time in nature
- Coaching

- Pets
- Attention training
- Gratitude
- Compassion
- Hope/optimism
- Courage/Facing fear
- Flexible thinking
- Humility
- Humor
- Altruism
- Self-control
- Self-efficacy
- Self-worth
- Self-awareness
- Acceptance
- Forgiveness
- Positive meaning
- Positive reframing
- Nurturing relationships
- Giving social support/Volunteering
- Positive role models
- Mindfulness/Meditation
- Yoga
- Morality
- Prayer
- Faith

Several resilience programs have been developed by integrating one or more of the elements from the above list. These programs have been tested among the following groups:

- Soldiers[277-283]
- Employees[249,275,284-290]
- Health care professionals [291-304,248]
- Patients[305-313]

I find every approach I have studied appealing in its own unique way. In general, programs that mainly educate have lower benefit compared to the programs that promote social interaction and build competence.[314]

After over a decade of work we have developed a program that over a period of time got the name SMART (Stress Management and Resiliency Training).

SMART

SMART is a structured approach to enhance self-awareness, focus, and a positive mindset based on integrating cutting-edge advances in neurosciences with timeless principles.

SMART is scientifically proven in about two dozen clinical studies to decrease symptoms of stress and anxiety and increase well-being, resilience, mindfulness, happiness, and positive health behaviors. You can access a gist of all our studies at the following link:
https://www.resiliencetrainer.com/curious-about-our-research/

SMART addresses two aspects of human experience—attention and interpretation.

Research shows that human attention instinctively focuses on threats and imperfections, especially in the past and the future. So, attention wanders; it ruminates. The human brain's default mode (dominated by default network) hosts mind wandering. Scientists have shockingly discovered that we spend half our day or more with a ruminative mind. This excessive 'dwell time' in the default mode correlates with symptoms of anxiety, depression, and attention deficit. It also fatigues our brain, one reason you might feel completely wiped out by 6 o'clock in the evening.

SMART offers a way out of this human dilemma by engaging the brain's focused mode—not only to experience more uplifting emotions but also to develop better focus, enhance creativity and productivity, better engagement at work, deeper relationships, and to find greater purpose in life.

SMART workshops help their participants with three closely integrated and inter-related steps:

1. Awareness—As a first step, participants develop a pragmatic understanding of the causes of stress and deficits in thriving. These are somewhat customized to the specific group that is being addressed. The participants learn three key neural vulnerabilities that generate and multiply our stress: focus, fatigue, and fear. This is shared in an evidence-based fashion while keeping the format simple, participatory, and fun. The self-awareness that emerges from these understandings empowers the individual to take the first step toward more fully realizing the potential of their brain.

2. Attention—As a next step, participants learn skills to develop an authentic, undistracted, and intentional presence. SMART fosters such engagement by training attention, a process that helps one discover greater novelty and meaning in the world. Trained attention finds deeper and more nurturing connections with people (friends, strangers, and loved ones alike), fulfills a greater purpose, and helps one direct and sustain deeper focus. Such an attention is flexible and relaxed, yet passionate and purposeful. The outcome of positive engagement is less fatigue, greater creativity and productivity, and a more empathetic disposition.

3. Attitude (resilient mindset)—SMART offers individuals a disciplined yet flexible focus to reframe their thinking with a more adaptive and pragmatic perspective that is conducive to a calm temperament as well as passionate engagement. Such perspective helps enhance gratitude focus, nurture greater compassion, creatively work with 'what is,' explore life's higher meaning, and strengthen forgiveness skills. The result is greater emotional intelligence, which in turn fosters more rewarding relationships, better emotional regulation, and thus enhanced abilities to deal with adversity.
The program shares application of these skills to daily life, both personal and professional.

If you wish, you can learn more about SMART at the following websites: resilientoption.com and resiliencetrainer.com.

I end our journey in this book with the same thoughts where we started, hopefully now with greater clarity and conviction:

Resilience is the core strength you use to lift the load of life.

Resilience is doing well when you shouldn't be doing well.

Just as you can learn math, music, and language, you can learn resilience.

Resilience skills upgrade and strengthen your neuronal networks by leveraging your brain's ability to change itself with experience.

The result: Enhanced resilience lifts every aspect of your life—physical, emotional, social, occupational, and spiritual.

You have a choice in how you experience each passing moment. Choose the resilient option, to live your day and your life to the fullest.

References

1.   Werner EE. High-risk children in young adulthood: a longitudinal study from birth to 32 years. The American journal of orthopsychiatry 1989;59:72-81.
2.   Werner EE. Resilience in development Current Directions in Psychological Science. Current Directions in Psychological Science 1995;4:81-5.
3.   Rutter M. Resilience in the face of adversity. Protective factors and resistance to psychiatric disorder. The British journal of psychiatry : the journal of mental science 1985;147:598-611.
4.   Kessler RC, Chiu WT, Demler O, Merikangas KR, Walters EE. Prevalence, severity, and comorbidity of 12-month DSM-IV disorders in the National Comorbidity Survey Replication. Arch Gen Psychiatry 2005;62:617-27.
5.   Amstadter AB, Aggen SH, Knudsen GP, Reichborn-Kjennerud T, Kendler KS. Potentially traumatic event exposure, posttraumatic stress disorder, and Axis I and II comorbidity in a population-based study of Norwegian young adults. Social psychiatry and psychiatric epidemiology 2013;48:215-23.
6.   Kessler RC, Berglund P, Demler O, Jin R, Merikangas KR, Walters EE. Lifetime prevalence and age-of-onset distributions of DSM-IV disorders in the National Comorbidity Survey Replication. Archives of general psychiatry 2005;62:593-602.
7.   Kessler RC, Sonnega A, Bromet E, Hughes M, Nelson CB. Posttraumatic stress disorder in the National Comorbidity Survey. Arch Gen Psychiatry 1995;52:1048-60.
8.   Norris FH, Tracy M, Galea S. Looking for resilience: understanding the longitudinal trajectories of responses to stress. Social science & medicine (1982) 2009;68:2190-8.
9.   Bonanno GA, Mancini AD, Horton JL, et al. Trajectories of trauma symptoms and resilience in deployed U.S. military service members: prospective cohort study. The British journal of psychiatry : the journal of mental science 2012;200:317-23.
10.   Workplace stress. AIS, 2018. (Accessed December 11th, 2018, 2018, at https://www.stress.org/workplace-stress/.)
11.   Gallup Daily: U.S. Employee Engagement. Gallup.com, 2018. (Accessed December 11th 2018, 2018, at https://news.gallup.com/poll/180404/gallup-daily-employee-engagement.aspx.)
12.   Poll: Most Americans Think Their Own Group Faces Discrimination. NPR, 2017. (Accessed December 11th, 2018, 2018, at https://www.npr.org/sections/health-shots/2017/10/24/559116373/poll-most-americans-think-their-own-group-faces-discrimination.)
13.   Rotenstein LS, Torre M, Ramos MA, et al. Prevalence of Burnout Among Physicians: A Systematic Review. Jama 2018;320:1131-50.
14.   Depression. WHO, 2018. (Accessed December 11th, 2018, 2018, at https://www.who.int/news-room/fact-sheets/detail/depression.)
15.   Suicide Statistics. American Foundation for Suicide Prevention, 2018. (Accessed December 9th, 2018, 2018, at https://afsp.org/about-suicide/suicide-statistics/.)
16.   Books Authored by Dr. Amit Sood. 2018. at https://static1.squarespace.com/static/5b1941a5620b852f7fe263ca/t/5b1adb22352f539420c12ffa/1528486691909/Books.pdf.)

17.   Smith-Osborne A, Whitehill Bolton K. Assessing resilience: a review of measures across the life course. J Evid Based Soc Work 2013;10:111-26.

18.   Windle G, Bennett KM, Noyes J. A methodological review of resilience measurement scales. Health Qual Life Outcomes 2011;9:8.

19.   Aburn G, Gott M, Hoare K. What is resilience? An Integrative Review of the empirical literature. J Adv Nurs 2016;72:980-1000.

20.   Shrivastava A, Desousa A. Resilience: A psychobiological construct for psychiatric disorders. Indian J Psychiatry 2016;58:38-43.

21.   Connor KM, Davidson JR. Development of a new resilience scale: the Connor-Davidson Resilience Scale (CD-RISC). Depress Anxiety 2003;18:76-82.

22.   Masten AS, Obradovic J. Competence and resilience in development. Annals of the New York Academy of Sciences 2006;1094:13-27.

23.   Rutter M. Psychosocial resilience and protective mechanisms. Am J Orthopsychiatry 1987;57:316-31.

24.   Whitson HE, Duan-Porter W, Schmader KE, Morey MC, Cohen HJ, Colon-Emeric CS. Physical Resilience in Older Adults: Systematic Review and Development of an Emerging Construct. J Gerontol A Biol Sci Med Sci 2016;71:489-95.

25.   Pietrzak RH, Goldstein MB, Malley JC, Rivers AJ, Johnson DC, Southwick SM. Risk and protective factors associated with suicidal ideation in veterans of Operations Enduring Freedom and Iraqi Freedom. Journal of affective disorders 2010;123:102-7.

26.   Masten AS. Ordinary magic. Resilience processes in development. The American psychologist 2001;56:227-38.

27.   Bonanno GA, Galea S, Bucciarelli A, Vlahov D. Psychological resilience after disaster: New York City in the aftermath of the September 11th terrorist attack. Psychol Sci 2006;17:181-6.

28.   Maguen S, Turcotte DM, Peterson AL, et al. Description of risk and resilience factors among military medical personnel before deployment to Iraq. Mil Med 2008;173:1-9.

29.   Masten AS, Tellegen A. Resilience in developmental psychopathology: contributions of the Project Competence Longitudinal Study. Development and psychopathology 2012;24:345-61.

30. Masten AS, Nuechterlein KH, Wright MO. Norman Garmezy (1918-2009). Am Psychol. 2011 Feb-Mar;66(2):140-1. doi: 10.1037/a0021246.

31.   Cicchetti D. The impact of social experience on neurobiological systems: illustration from a constructivist view of child maltreatment. Cognitive Development 2002;17:1407-28.

32.   Luthar SS. Vulnerability and resilience: a study of high-risk adolescents. Child development 1991;62:600-16.

33.   Luthar SS, Sexton CC. Maternal drug abuse versus maternal depression: vulnerability and resilience among school-age and adolescent offspring. Development and psychopathology 2007;19:205-25.

34.   Cutuli JJ, Desjardins CD, Herbers JE, et al. Academic achievement trajectories of homeless and highly mobile students: resilience in the context of chronic and acute risk. Child development 2013;84:841-57.

35. Masten AS. Resilience in children threatened by extreme adversity: frameworks for research, practice, and translational synergy. Development and psychopathology 2011;23:493-506.

36. Masten AS, Narayan AJ. Child development in the context of disaster, war, and terrorism: pathways of risk and resilience. Annual review of psychology 2012;63:227-57.

37. Wells RD, Schwebel AI. Chronically ill children and their mothers: predictors of resilience and vulnerability to hospitalization and surgical stress. Journal of developmental and behavioral pediatrics : JDBP 1987;8:83-9.

38. Masten AS. Resilience in developing systems: progress and promise as the fourth wave rises. Development and psychopathology 2007;19:921-30.

39. Steinheuser V, Ackermann K, Schonfeld P, Schwabe L. Stress and the city: impact of urban upbringing on the (re)activity of the hypothalamus-pituitary-adrenal axis. Psychosomatic medicine 2014;76:678-85.

40. Gralinski-Bakker JH, Hauser ST, Stott C, Billings RL, Allen JP. Markers of Resilience and Risk: Adult Lives in a Vulnerable Population. Research in human development 2004;1:291-326.

41. Vaillant GE, Davis JT. Social/emotional intelligence and midlife resilience in schoolboys with low tested intelligence. The American journal of orthopsychiatry 2000;70:215-22.

42. Burt KB, Paysnick AA. Resilience in the transition to adulthood. Development and psychopathology 2012;24:493-505.

43. Gouzman J, Cohen M, Ben-Zur H, et al. Resilience and psychosocial adjustment in digestive system cancer. J Clin Psychol Med Settings 2015;22:1-13.

44. MacDermott D. Psychological hardiness and meaning making as protection against sequelae in veterans of the wars in Iraq and Afghanistan. Int J Emerg Ment Health 2010;12:199-206.

45. Vieselmeyer J, Holguin J, Mezulis A. The Role of Resilience and Gratitude in Posttraumatic Stress and Growth Following a Campus Shooting. Psychol Trauma 2016.

46. Bonanno GA, Galea S, Bucciarelli A, Vlahov D. What predicts psychological resilience after disaster? The role of demographics, resources, and life stress. J Consult Clin Psychol 2007;75:671-82.

47. Bonanno GA, Kennedy P, Galatzer-Levy IR, Lude P, Elfstrom ML. Trajectories of resilience, depression, and anxiety following spinal cord injury. Rehabilitation psychology 2012;57:236-47.

48. Chochovski J, Moss SA, Charman DP. Recovery after unsuccessful in vitro fertilization: the complex role of resilience and marital relationships. J Psychosom Obstet Gynaecol 2013;34:122-8.

49. Bonanno GA, Diminich ED. Annual Research Review: Positive adjustment to adversity--trajectories of minimal-impact resilience and emergent resilience. J Child Psychol Psychiatry 2013;54:378-401.

50. Sood A. Mindfulness Redesigned for the Twenty-First Century: Global Center for Resiliency and Wellbeing; 2018.

51. Montori V. Why we revolt: A patient revolution for careful and kind care: The Patient Revolution; 2017.

52. Duan W, Guo P, Gan P. Relationships among Trait Resilience, Virtues, Post-traumatic Stress Disorder, and Post-traumatic Growth. PLoS One 2015;10:e0125707.

53. Gloria CT, Steinhardt MA. Relationships Among Positive Emotions, Coping, Resilience and Mental Health. Stress Health 2016;32:145-56.

54. Mayordomo T, Viguer P, Sales A, Satorres E, Melendez JC. Resilience and Coping as Predictors of Well-Being in Adults. J Psychol 2016:1-13.

55. Chinese scientist claims world's first gene-edited babies, amid denial from hospital and international outcry. CNN.com, 2018. (Accessed December 8th, 2018, 2018, at https://www.cnn.com/2018/11/26/health/china-crispr-gene-editing-twin-babies-first-intl/index.html.)

56. Keeney RL. Personal Decisions Are the Leading Cause of Death. Operations Research 2008;56:1335-47.

57. Conner TS, Brookie KL, Richardson AC, Polak MA. On carrots and curiosity: eating fruit and vegetables is associated with greater flourishing in daily life. British journal of health psychology 2015;20:413-27.

58. Hamer M. Psychosocial stress and cardiovascular disease risk: the role of physical activity. Psychosomatic medicine 2012;74:896-903.

59. Hamer M, Endrighi R, Poole L. Physical activity, stress reduction, and mood: insight into immunological mechanisms. Methods in molecular biology (Clifton, NJ) 2012;934:89-102.

60. Lesani A, Mohammadpoorasl A, Javadi M, Esfeh JM, Fakhari A. Eating breakfast, fruit and vegetable intake and their relation with happiness in college students. Eating and weight disorders : EWD 2016;21:645-51.

61. Mujcic R, A JO. Evolution of Well-Being and Happiness After Increases in Consumption of Fruit and Vegetables. American journal of public health 2016;106:1504-10.

62. Shin JE, Kim JK. How a Good Sleep Predicts Life Satisfaction: The Role of Zero-Sum Beliefs About Happiness. Frontiers in psychology 2018;9:1589.

63. Sithey G, Wen LM, Kelly P, Li M. Association between Sleep Duration and Self-Reported Health Status: Findings from the Bhutan's Gross National Happiness Study. Journal of clinical sleep medicine : JCSM : official publication of the American Academy of Sleep Medicine 2017;13:33-8.

64. Fotuhi M, Do D, Jack C. Modifiable factors that alter the size of the hippocampus with ageing. Nature reviews Neurology 2012;8:189-202.

65. Joo EY, Kim H, Suh S, Hong SB. Hippocampal substructural vulnerability to sleep disturbance and cognitive impairment in patients with chronic primary insomnia: magnetic resonance imaging morphometry. Sleep 2014;37:1189-98.

66. Sexton CE, Storsve AB, Walhovd KB, Johansen-Berg H, Fjell AM. Poor sleep quality is associated with increased cortical atrophy in community-dwelling adults. Neurology 2014;83:967-73.

67. Yau SY, Lau BW, So KF. Adult hippocampal neurogenesis: a possible way how physical exercise counteracts stress. Cell transplantation 2011;20:99-111.

68. Berger SL, Kouzarides T, Shiekhattar R, Shilatifard A. An operational definition of epigenetics. Genes & development 2009;23:781-3.

69. Zannas AS, West AE. Epigenetics and the regulation of stress vulnerability and resilience. Neuroscience 2014;264:157-70.

70.   Smith JA, Zhao W, Wang X, et al. Neighborhood characteristics influence DNA methylation of genes involved in stress response and inflammation: The Multi-Ethnic Study of Atherosclerosis. Epigenetics 2017;12:662-73.

71.   Bakusic J, Schaufeli W, Claes S, Godderis L. Stress, burnout and depression: A systematic review on DNA methylation mechanisms. Journal of psychosomatic research 2017;92:34-44.

72.   Zannas AS, Chrousos GP. Epigenetic programming by stress and glucocorticoids along the human lifespan. Molecular psychiatry 2017;22:640-6.

73.   Chen Q, Yan W, Duan E. Epigenetic inheritance of acquired traits through sperm RNAs and sperm RNA modifications. Nature reviews Genetics 2016;17:733-43.

74.   Short AK, Fennell KA, Perreau VM, et al. Elevated paternal glucocorticoid exposure alters the small noncoding RNA profile in sperm and modifies anxiety and depressive phenotypes in the offspring. Translational psychiatry 2016;6:e837.

75.   Wei Y, Schatten H, Sun QY. Environmental epigenetic inheritance through gametes and implications for human reproduction. Human reproduction update 2015;21:194-208.

76.   Dudley KJ, Li X, Kobor MS, Kippin TE, Bredy TW. Epigenetic mechanisms mediating vulnerability and resilience to psychiatric disorders. Neuroscience and biobehavioral reviews 2011;35:1544-51.

77.   Kim-Cohen J, Turkewitz R. Resilience and measured gene-environment interactions. Development and psychopathology 2012;24:1297-306.

78.   Bouchard TJ, Jr. Genes, environment, and personality. Science (New York, NY) 1994;264:1700-1.

79.   Bouchard TJ, Jr., Lykken DT, McGue M, Segal NL, Tellegen A. Sources of human psychological differences: the Minnesota Study of Twins Reared Apart. Science (New York, NY) 1990;250:223-8.

80.   Fredrickson BL, Grewen KM, Algoe SB, et al. Psychological well-being and the human conserved transcriptional response to adversity. PloS one 2015;10:e0121839.

81.   Kanherkar RR, Bhatia-Dey N, Csoka AB. Epigenetics across the human lifespan. Frontiers in cell and developmental biology 2014;2:49.

82.   Morales-Lara D, De-la-Pena C, Murillo-Rodriguez E. Dad's Snoring May Have Left Molecular Scars in Your DNA: the Emerging Role of Epigenetics in Sleep Disorders. Molecular neurobiology 2017.

83.   Peedicayil J. The role of epigenetics in social psychiatry. The International journal of social psychiatry 2017;63:14-20.

84.   Pickersgill M, Niewohner J, Muller R, Martin P, Cunningham-Burley S. Mapping the new molecular landscape: social dimensions of epigenetics. New genetics and society 2013;32:429-47.

85.   Zannas AS. Gene-environment Interactions in Late Life: Linking Psychosocial Stress with Brain Aging. Current neuropharmacology 2018;16:327-33.

86.   Caspi A, Sugden K, Moffitt TE, et al. Influence of life stress on depression: moderation by a polymorphism in the 5-HTT gene. Science (New York, NY) 2003;301:386-9.

87.   Munafo MR, Clark TG, Roberts KH, Johnstone EC. Neuroticism mediates the association of the serotonin transporter gene with lifetime major depression. Neuropsychobiology 2006;53:1-8.

88.   Stein MB, Campbell-Sills L, Gelernter J. Genetic variation in 5HTTLPR is associated with emotional resilience. American journal of medical genetics Part B, Neuropsychiatric genetics : the official publication of the International Society of Psychiatric Genetics 2009;150b:900-6.

89.   Jonassaint CR, Ashley-Koch A, Whitfield KE, et al. The serotonin transporter gene polymorphism (5HTTLPR) moderates the effect of adolescent environmental conditions on self-esteem in young adulthood: a structural equation modeling approach. Biological psychology 2012;91:111-9.

90.   Haberstick BC, Boardman JD, Wagner B, et al. Depression, Stressful Life Events, and the Impact of Variation in the Serotonin Transporter: Findings from the National Longitudinal Study of Adolescent to Adult Health (Add Health). PloS one 2016;11:e0148373.

91.   Barr CS, Newman TK, Shannon C, et al. Rearing condition and rh5-HTTLPR interact to influence limbic-hypothalamic-pituitary-adrenal axis response to stress in infant macaques. Biological psychiatry 2004;55:733-8.

92.   Gotlib IH, Joormann J, Minor KL, Hallmayer J. HPA axis reactivity: a mechanism underlying the associations among 5-HTTLPR, stress, and depression. Biological psychiatry 2008;63:847-51.

93.   Oo KZ, Aung YK, Jenkins MA, Win AK. Associations of 5HTTLPR polymorphism with major depressive disorder and alcohol dependence: A systematic review and meta-analysis. The Australian and New Zealand journal of psychiatry 2016;50:842-57.

94.   Petito A, Altamura M, Iuso S, et al. The Relationship between Personality Traits, the 5HTT Polymorphisms, and the Occurrence of Anxiety and Depressive Symptoms in Elite Athletes. PloS one 2016;11:e0156601.

95.   Bowes L, Jaffee SR. Biology, genes, and resilience: toward a multidisciplinary approach. Trauma, violence & abuse 2013;14:195-208.

96.   Cruz-Fuentes CS, Benjet C, Martinez-Levy GA, Perez-Molina A, Briones-Velasco M, Suarez-Gonzalez J. BDNF Met66 modulates the cumulative effect of psychosocial childhood adversities on major depression in adolescents. Brain and behavior 2014;4:290-7.

97.   Daskalakis NP, Bagot RC, Parker KJ, Vinkers CH, de Kloet ER. The three-hit concept of vulnerability and resilience: toward understanding adaptation to early-life adversity outcome. Psychoneuroendocrinology 2013;38:1858-73.

98.   Dunn EC, Solovieff N, Lowe SR, et al. Interaction between genetic variants and exposure to Hurricane Katrina on post-traumatic stress and post-traumatic growth: a prospective analysis of low income adults. Journal of affective disorders 2014;152-154:243-9.

99.   Lyons MJ, Genderson M, Grant MD, et al. Gene-environment interaction of ApoE genotype and combat exposure on PTSD. American journal of medical genetics Part B, Neuropsychiatric genetics : the official publication of the International Society of Psychiatric Genetics 2013;162b:762-9.

100. Manuck SB, McCaffery JM. Gene-environment interaction. Annual review of psychology 2014;65:41-70.

101. Watkins LE, Han S, Harpaz-Rotem I, et al. FKBP5 polymorphisms, childhood abuse, and PTSD symptoms: Results from the National Health and Resilience in Veterans Study. Psychoneuroendocrinology 2016;69:98-105.

102. Olsson CA, Byrnes GB, Anney RJ, et al. COMT Val(158)Met and 5HTTLPR functional loci interact to predict persistence of anxiety across adolescence: results from the Victorian Adolescent Health Cohort Study. Genes, brain, and behavior 2007;6:647-52.

103. Wong ML, Arcos-Burgos M, Liu S, et al. The PHF21B gene is associated with major depression and modulates the stress response. Molecular psychiatry 2017;22:1015-25.

104. Cerda M, Sagdeo A, Johnson J, Galea S. Genetic and environmental influences on psychiatric comorbidity: a systematic review. Journal of affective disorders 2010;126:14-38.

105. Kohrt BA, Worthman CM, Ressler KJ, et al. Cross-cultural gene- environment interactions in depression, post-traumatic stress disorder, and the cortisol awakening response: FKBP5 polymorphisms and childhood trauma in South Asia. International review of psychiatry (Abingdon, England) 2015;27:180-96.

106. Zannas AS, Binder EB. Gene-environment interactions at the FKBP5 locus: sensitive periods, mechanisms and pleiotropism. Genes, brain, and behavior 2014;13:25-37.

107. Crum AJ, Akinola M, Turnwald BP, Kaptchuk TJ, Hall KT. Catechol-O-Methyltransferase moderates effect of stress mindset on affect and cognition. PloS one 2018;13:e0195883.

108. Rutter M. Resilience as a dynamic concept. Development and psychopathology 2012;24:335-44.

109. McEwen BS. In pursuit of resilience: stress, epigenetics, and brain plasticity. Annals of the New York Academy of Sciences 2016;1373:56-64.

110. McEwen BS. Allostasis and the Epigenetics of Brain and Body Health Over the Life Course: The Brain on Stress. JAMA psychiatry 2017.

111. Osorio C, Probert T, Jones E, Young AH, Robbins I. Adapting to Stress: Understanding the Neurobiology of Resilience. Behavioral medicine (Washington, DC) 2016:1-16.

112. Wu G, Feder A, Cohen H, et al. Understanding resilience. Frontiers in behavioral neuroscience 2013;7:10.

113. Morgan CA, 3rd, Rasmusson AM, Wang S, Hoyt G, Hauger RL, Hazlett G. Neuropeptide-Y, cortisol, and subjective distress in humans exposed to acute stress: replication and extension of previous report. Biological psychiatry 2002;52:136-42.

114. Morgan CA, 3rd, Wang S, Southwick SM, et al. Plasma neuropeptide-Y concentrations in humans exposed to military survival training. Biological psychiatry 2000;47:902-9.

115. dos Santos VV, Santos DB, Lach G, et al. Neuropeptide Y (NPY) prevents depressive-like behavior, spatial memory deficits and oxidative stress following amyloid-beta (Abeta(1-40)) administration in mice. Behavioural brain research 2013;244:107-15.

116. Serova LI, Tillinger A, Alaluf LG, Laukova M, Keegan K, Sabban EL. Single intranasal neuropeptide Y infusion attenuates development of PTSD-like symptoms to traumatic stress in rats. Neuroscience 2013;236:298-312.

117. Nair KS, Rizza RA, O'Brien P, et al. DHEA in elderly women and DHEA or testosterone in elderly men. The New England journal of medicine 2006;355:1647-59.

118. Curtin CG, Parker JP. Foundations of resilience thinking. Conservation biology : the journal of the Society for Conservation Biology 2014;28:912-23.

119. Farber EW, Schwartz JA, Schaper PE, Moonen DJ, McDaniel JS. Resilience factors associated with adaptation to HIV disease. Psychosomatics 2000;41:140-6.

120. Kobasa SC. Stressful life events, personality, and health: an inquiry into hardiness. J Pers Soc Psychol 1979;37:1-11.

121. Bartone PT, Ursano RJ, Wright KM, Ingraham LH. The impact of a military air disaster on the health of assistance workers. A prospective study. J Nerv Ment Dis 1989;177:317-28.

122. Ford IW, Eklund RC, Gordon S. An examination of psychosocial variables moderating the relationship between life stress and injury time-loss among athletes of a high standard. J Sports Sci 2000;18:301-12.

123. Lang A, Goulet C, Amsel R. Lang and Goulet Hardiness Scale: development and testing on bereaved parents following the death of their fetus/infant. Death Stud 2003;27:851-80.

124. Northouse LL, Mood D, Kershaw T, et al. Quality of life of women with recurrent breast cancer and their family members. J Clin Oncol 2002;20:4050-64.

125. Williams D, Lawler KA. Stress and illness in low-income women: the roles of hardiness, John Henryism, and race. Women Health 2001;32:61-75.

126. Ruff G, Korchin S. Psychological respones of the Mercury astronauts to stress, in the Threat of Impending Disaster. . Cambridge, Mass: MIT Press; 1964.

127. Johnsen BH, Eid J, Laberg JC, Thayer JF. The effect of sensitization and coping style on post-traumatic stress symptoms and quality of life: two longitudinal studies. Scand J Psychol 2002;43:181-8.

128. Regehr C, Hill J, Glancy GD. Individual predictors of traumatic reactions in firefighters. J Nerv Ment Dis 2000;188:333-9.

129. Soet JE, Brack GA, DiIorio C. Prevalence and predictors of women's experience of psychological trauma during childbirth. Birth 2003;30:36-46.

130. Livanou M, Basoglu M, Marks IM, et al. Beliefs, sense of control and treatment outcome in post-traumatic stress disorder. Psychol Med 2002;32:157-65.

131. Valentiner DP, Foa E, Riggs DS, Gershuny BS. Coping strategies and posttraumatic stress disorder in female victims of sexual and nonsexual assault. J Abnorm Psychol 1996;105:455-8.

132. Ai AL, Cascio T, Santangelo LK, Evans-Campbell T. Hope, meaning, and growth following the September 11, 2001, terrorist attacks. J Interpers Violence 2005;20:523-48.

133. Ai AL, Tice TN, Peterson C, Huang B. Prayers, spiritual support, and positive attitudes in coping with the September 11 national crisis. J Pers 2005;73:763-91.

134. Basoglu M, Mineka S, Paker M, Aker T, Livanou M, Gok S. Psychological preparedness for trauma as a protective factor in survivors of torture. Psychol Med 1997;27:1421-33.

135. Brewin CR, Andrews B, Valentine JD. Meta-analysis of risk factors for posttraumatic stress disorder in trauma-exposed adults. J Consult Clin Psychol 2000;68:748-66.

136. King LA, King DW, Fairbank JA, Keane TM, Adams GA. Resilience-recovery factors in post-traumatic stress disorder among female and male Vietnam veterans: hardiness, postwar social support, and additional stressful life events. J Pers Soc Psychol 1998;74:420-34.

137. Turner SW, Bowie C, Dunn G, Shapo L, Yule W. Mental health of Kosovan Albanian refugees in the UK. The British journal of psychiatry : the journal of mental science 2003;182:444-8.

138. Perry S, Difede J, Musngi G, Frances AJ, Jacobsberg L. Predictors of posttraumatic stress disorder after burn injury. Am J Psychiatry 1992;149:931-5.

139. Charney DS. Psychobiological mechanisms of resilience and vulnerability: implications for successful adaptation to extreme stress. Am J Psychiatry 2004;161:195-216.

140. Wulff K, Donato D, Lurie N. What is health resilience and how can we build it? Annual review of public health 2015;36:361-74.

141. Neave N, Wolfson S. Testosterone, territoriality, and the 'home advantage'. Physiology & behavior 2003;78:269-75.

142. Survey of American Fears 2018. Chapman.edu, 2018. (Accessed December 9th, 2018, 2018, at https://www.chapman.edu/wilkinson/research-centers/babbie-center/_files/fear-2018/2018-Fear-Campaign-Summary.pdf.)

143. Hwang MJ, Cheong HK, Kim JH, Koo YS, Yun HY. Ambient air quality and subjective stress level using Community Health Survey data in Korea. Epidemiology and health 2018;40:e2018028.

144. Vanman EJ, Baker R, Tobin SJ. The burden of online friends: the effects of giving up Facebook on stress and well-being. The Journal of social psychology 2018;158:496-507.

145. Bonanno GA. Loss, trauma, and human resilience: have we underestimated the human capacity to thrive after extremely aversive events? The American psychologist 2004;59:20-8.

146. Stress Management and Resilience Training. GCRW, 2018. (Accessed December 9th, 2018, 2018, at https://www.resiliencetrainer.com.)

147. Resilience research. GCRW, 2018. (Accessed December 9th, 2018, 2018, at https://www.resiliencetrainer.com/curious-about-our-research/.)

148. Adamo SA. Stress responses sculpt the insect immune system, optimizing defense in an ever-changing world. Developmental and comparative immunology 2017;66:24-32.

149. Shah AJ, Lampert R, Goldberg J, Veledar E, Bremner JD, Vaccarino V. Posttraumatic stress disorder and impaired autonomic modulation in male twins. Biological psychiatry 2013;73:1103-10.

150. Blix E, Perski A, Berglund H, Savic I. Long-term occupational stress is associated with regional reductions in brain tissue volumes. PloS one 2013;8:e64065.

151. Savic I. Structural changes of the brain in relation to occupational stress. Cerebral cortex (New York, NY : 1991) 2015;25:1554-64.

152. Goldfarb EV, Frobose MI, Cools R, Phelps EA. Stress and Cognitive Flexibility: Cortisol Increases Are Associated with Enhanced Updating but Impaired Switching. Journal of cognitive neuroscience 2017;29:14-24.

153. Vogel S, Klumpers F, Schroder TN, et al. Stress Induces a Shift Towards Striatum-Dependent Stimulus-Response Learning via the Mineralocorticoid Receptor.

Neuropsychopharmacology : official publication of the American College of Neuropsychopharmacology 2017;42:1262-71.

154. Brydon L, Walker C, Wawrzyniak AJ, Chart H, Steptoe A. Dispositional optimism and stress-induced changes in immunity and negative mood. Brain, behavior, and immunity 2009;23:810-6.

155. Nakata A. Psychosocial job stress and immunity: a systematic review. Methods in molecular biology (Clifton, NJ) 2012;934:39-75.

156. Truckenmiller ME, Bonneau RH, Norbury CC. Stress presents a problem for dendritic cells: corticosterone and the fate of MHC class I antigen processing and presentation. Brain, behavior, and immunity 2006;20:210-8.

157. Segerstrom SC, Miller GE. Psychological stress and the human immune system: a meta-analytic study of 30 years of inquiry. Psychol Bull 2004;130:601-30.

158. Steptoe A, Hamer M, Chida Y. The effects of acute psychological stress on circulating inflammatory factors in humans: a review and meta-analysis. Brain Behav Immun 2007;21:901-12.

159. Thrall G, Lane D, Carroll D, Lip GY. A systematic review of the effects of acute psychological stress and physical activity on haemorheology, coagulation, fibrinolysis and platelet reactivity: Implications for the pathogenesis of acute coronary syndromes. Thromb Res 2007;120:819-47.

160. Sumner JA, Kubzansky LD, Kabrhel C, et al. Associations of Trauma Exposure and Posttraumatic Stress Symptoms With Venous Thromboembolism Over 22 Years in Women. Journal of the American Heart Association 2016;5.

161. Kershaw KN, Lane-Cordova AD, Carnethon MR, Tindle HA, Liu K. Chronic Stress and Endothelial Dysfunction: The Multi-Ethnic Study of Atherosclerosis (MESA). American journal of hypertension 2017;30:75-80.

162. Clark MM, Jenkins SM, Hagen PT, et al. High Stress and Negative Health Behaviors: A Five-Year Wellness Center Member Cohort Study. Journal of occupational and environmental medicine 2016;58:868-73.

163. Thurston IB, Hardin R, Kamody RC, Herbozo S, Kaufman C. The moderating role of resilience on the relationship between perceived stress and binge eating symptoms among young adult women. Eating behaviors 2018;29:114-9.

164. Dianatinasab M, Fararouei M, Mohammadianpanah M, Zare-Bandamiri M, Rezaianzadeh A. Hair Coloring, Stress, and Smoking Increase the Risk of Breast Cancer: A Case-Control Study. Clinical breast cancer 2017;17:650-9.

165. Song H, Fang F, Tomasson G, et al. Association of Stress-Related Disorders With Subsequent Autoimmune Disease. Jama 2018;319:2388-400.

166. Kotlega D, Golab-Janowska M, Masztalewicz M, Ciecwiez S, Nowacki P. The emotional stress and risk of ischemic stroke. Neurologia i neurochirurgia polska 2016;50:265-70.

167. Lampert R. Mental Stress and Ventricular Arrhythmias. Current cardiology reports 2016;18:118.

168. Epel ES, McEwen BS, Ickovics JR. Embodying psychological thriving: physical thriving in response to threat. Journal of Social Issues 1998;54:301-22.

169. Innes KE, Vincent HK, Taylor AG. Chronic stress and insulin resistance-related indices of cardiovascular disease risk, part 2: a potential role for mind-body therapies. Altern Ther Health Med 2007;13:44-51.

170. Chan YE, Bai YM, Hsu JW, et al. Post-traumatic Stress Disorder and Risk of Parkinson Disease: A Nationwide Longitudinal Study. The American journal of geriatric psychiatry : official journal of the American Association for Geriatric Psychiatry 2017;25:917-23.

171. Mravec B, Horvathova L, Padova A. Brain Under Stress and Alzheimer's Disease. Cellular and molecular neurobiology 2018;38:73-84.

172. Sindi S, Kareholt I, Solomon A, Hooshmand B, Soininen H, Kivipelto M. Midlife work-related stress is associated with late-life cognition. Journal of neurology 2017;264:1996-2002.

173. Agrigoroaei S, Lee-Attardo A, Lachman ME. Stress and Subjective Age: Those With Greater Financial Stress Look Older. Research on aging 2017;39:1075-99.

174. Kivimaki M, Virtanen M, Elovainio M, Kouvonen A, Vaananen A, Vahtera J. Work stress in the etiology of coronary heart disease - a meta-analysis. Scand J Work Environ Health 2006;32:431-42.

175. Krantz DS, McCeney MK. Effects of psychological and social factors on organic disease: a critical assessment of research on coronary heart disease. Annual review of psychology 2002;53:341-69.

176. Antoni MH, Lutgendorf SK, Cole SW, et al. The influence of bio-behavioural factors on tumour biology: pathways and mechanisms. Nat Rev Cancer 2006;6:240-8.

177. Leserman J, Petitto JM, Gu H, et al. Progression to AIDS, a clinical AIDS condition and mortality: psychosocial and physiological predictors. Psychol Med 2002;32:1059-73.

178. Pereira DB, Antoni MH, Danielson A, et al. Stress as a predictor of symptomatic genital herpes virus recurrence in women with human immunodeficiency virus. J Psychosom Res 2003;54:237-44.

179. Duijts SF, Zeegers MP, Borne BV. The association between stressful life events and breast cancer risk: a meta-analysis. Int J Cancer 2003;107:1023-9.

180. Heffner KL, Loving TJ, Robles TF, Kiecolt-Glaser JK. Examining psychosocial factors related to cancer incidence and progression: in search of the silver lining. Brain Behav Immun 2003;17 Suppl 1:S109-11.

181. Siegrist J, Li J. Work Stress and Altered Biomarkers: A Synthesis of Findings Based on the Effort-Reward Imbalance Model. International journal of environmental research and public health 2017;14.

182. Jacob L, Haro JM, Koyanagi A. Post-traumatic stress symptoms are associated with physical multimorbidity: Findings from the Adult Psychiatric Morbidity Survey 2007. Journal of affective disorders 2018;232:385-92.

183. Stewart DE, Yuen T. A systematic review of resilience in the physically ill. Psychosomatics 2011;52:199-209.

184. Rosenberg AR, Syrjala KL, Martin PJ, et al. Resilience, health, and quality of life among long-term survivors of hematopoietic cell transplantation. Cancer 2015;121:4250-7.

185. Schumacher A, Sauerland C, Silling G, Berdel WE, Stelljes M. Resilience in patients after allogeneic stem cell transplantation. Support Care Cancer 2014;22:487-93.

186. Strauss B, Brix C, Fischer S, et al. The influence of resilience on fatigue in cancer patients undergoing radiation therapy (RT). J Cancer Res Clin Oncol 2007;133:511-8.

187. Groenvold M, Petersen MA, Idler E, Bjorner JB, Fayers PM, Mouridsen HT. Psychological distress and fatigue predicted recurrence and survival in primary breast cancer patients. Breast Cancer Res Treat 2007;105:209-19.

188. Harris LN, Bauer MR, Wiley JF, et al. Chronic and episodic stress predict physical symptom bother following breast cancer diagnosis. Journal of behavioral medicine 2017;40:875-85.

189. Gotay CC, Isaacs P, Pagano I. Quality of life in patients who survive a dire prognosis compared to control cancer survivors. Psychooncology 2004;13:882-92.

190. Eicher M, Matzka M, Dubey C, White K. Resilience in adult cancer care: an integrative literature review. Oncol Nurs Forum 2015;42:E3-16.

191. Matzka M, Mayer H, Kock-Hodi S, et al. Relationship between Resilience, Psychological Distress and Physical Activity in Cancer Patients: A Cross-Sectional Observation Study. PLoS One 2016;11:e0154496.

192. Lu W, Wang Z, You X. Physiological Responses to Repeated Stress in Individuals with High and Low Trait Resilience. Biol Psychol 2016.

193. Hagstrom E, Norlund F, Stebbins A, et al. Psychosocial stress and major cardiovascular events in patients with stable coronary heart disease. Journal of internal medicine 2018;283:83-92.

194. Hopkins KD, Shepherd CC, Taylor CL, Zubrick SR. Relationships between Psychosocial Resilience and Physical Health Status of Western Australian Urban Aboriginal Youth. PLoS One 2015;10:e0145382.

195. Ma LC, Chang HJ, Liu YM, et al. The relationship between health-promoting behaviors and resilience in patients with chronic kidney disease. ScientificWorldJournal 2013;2013:124973.

196. Robottom BJ, Gruber-Baldini AL, Anderson KE, et al. What determines resilience in patients with Parkinson's disease? Parkinsonism Relat Disord 2012;18:174-7.

197. Hackett RA, Steptoe A. Type 2 diabetes mellitus and psychological stress - a modifiable risk factor. Nature reviews Endocrinology 2017;13:547-60.

198. Yi JP, Vitaliano PP, Smith RE, Yi JC, Weinger K. The role of resilience on psychological adjustment and physical health in patients with diabetes. Br J Health Psychol 2007.

199. Puig-Perez S, Hackett RA, Salvador A, Steptoe A. Optimism moderates psychophysiological responses to stress in older people with Type 2 diabetes. Psychophysiology 2017;54:536-43.

200. Pesantes MA, Lazo-Porras M, Abu Dabrh AM, et al. Resilience in Vulnerable Populations With Type 2 Diabetes Mellitus and Hypertension: A Systematic Review and Meta-analysis. Can J Cardiol 2015;31:1180-8.

201. Nawaz A, Malik JA, Batool A. Relationship between resilience and quality of life in diabetics. J Coll Physicians Surg Pak 2014;24:670-5.

202. Wang Y, Chen X, Gong J, Yan Y. Relationships Between Stress, Negative Emotions, Resilience, and Smoking: Testing a Moderated Mediation Model. Subst Use Misuse 2016;51:427-38.

203. Hodder RK, Daly J, Freund M, Bowman J, Hazell T, Wiggers J. A school-based resilience intervention to decrease tobacco, alcohol and marijuana use in high school students. BMC Public Health 2011;11:722.

204. Alschuler KN, Kratz AL, Ehde DM. Resilience and vulnerability in individuals with chronic pain and physical disability. Rehabilitation psychology 2016;61:7-18.

205. Losoi H, Waljas M, Turunen S, et al. Resilience is associated with fatigue after mild traumatic brain injury. J Head Trauma Rehabil 2015;30:E24-32.

206. Shields GS, Doty D, Shields RH, Gower G, Slavich GM, Yonelinas AP. Recent life stress exposure is associated with poorer long-term memory, working memory, and self-reported memory. Stress (Amsterdam, Netherlands) 2017;20:598-607.

207. Mohlenhoff BS, O'Donovan A, Weiner MW, Neylan TC. Dementia Risk in Posttraumatic Stress Disorder: the Relevance of Sleep-Related Abnormalities in Brain Structure, Amyloid, and Inflammation. Current psychiatry reports 2017;19:89.

208. Lavoie J, Pereira LC, Talwar V. Children's Physical Resilience Outcomes: Meta-Analysis of Vulnerability and Protective Factors. J Pediatr Nurs 2016.

209. Innes SI. The relationship between levels of resilience and coping styles in chiropractic students and perceived levels of stress and well-being. J Chiropr Educ 2016.

210. Tempski P, Santos IS, Mayer FB, et al. Relationship among Medical Student Resilience, Educational Environment and Quality of Life. PLoS One 2015;10:e0131535.

211. Schure MB, Odden M, Goins RT. The association of resilience with mental and physical health among older American Indians: the Native Elder Care Study. American Indian and Alaska native mental health research (Online) 2013;20:27-41.

212. Green KT, Calhoun PS, Dennis MF, Beckham JC. Exploration of the resilience construct in posttraumatic stress disorder severity and functional correlates in military combat veterans who have served since September 11, 2001. The Journal of clinical psychiatry 2010;71:823-30.

213. Manning LK, Carr DC, Kail BL. Do Higher Levels of Resilience Buffer the Deleterious Impact of Chronic Illness on Disability in Later Life? Gerontologist 2016;56:514-24.

214. Duan-Porter W, Cohen HJ, Demark-Wahnefried W, et al. Physical resilience of older cancer survivors: An emerging concept. J Geriatr Oncol 2016.

215. Moore RC, Eyler LT, Mausbach BT, et al. Complex interplay between health and successful aging: role of perceived stress, resilience, and social support. Am J Geriatr Psychiatry 2015;23:622-32.

216. Tian X, Gao Q, Li G, et al. Resilience is associated with low psychological distress in renal transplant recipients. Gen Hosp Psychiatry 2016;39:86-90.

217. Pakalniskiene V, Viliuniene R, Hilbig J. Patients' resilience and distress over time: Is resilience a prognostic indicator of treatment? Compr Psychiatry 2016;69:88-99.

218. Cuhadar D, Tanriverdi D, Pehlivan M, Kurnaz G, Alkan S. Determination of the psychiatric symptoms and psychological resilience levels of hematopoietic stem cell transplant patients and their relatives. Eur J Cancer Care (Engl) 2016;25:112-21.

219. Wu WW, Tsai SY, Liang SY, Liu CY, Jou ST, Berry DL. The Mediating Role of Resilience on Quality of Life and Cancer Symptom Distress in Adolescent Patients With Cancer. J Pediatr Oncol Nurs 2015;32:304-13.

220. Simpson GK, Dall'Armi L, Roydhouse JK, et al. Does Resilience Mediate Carer Distress After Head and Neck Cancer? Cancer Nurs 2015;38:E30-6.

221. Tian J, Hong JS. Assessment of the relationship between resilience and quality of life in patients with digestive cancer. World J Gastroenterol 2014;20:18439-44.

222. Lim JW, Shon EJ, Paek M, Daly B. The dyadic effects of coping and resilience on psychological distress for cancer survivor couples. Support Care Cancer 2014;22:3209-17.

223. Cohen M, Baziliansky S, Beny A. The association of resilience and age in individuals with colorectal cancer: an exploratory cross-sectional study. J Geriatr Oncol 2014;5:33-9.

224. Min JA, Yoon S, Lee CU, et al. Psychological resilience contributes to low emotional distress in cancer patients. Support Care Cancer 2013;21:2469-76.

225. Kim KR, Song YY, Park JY, et al. The relationship between psychosocial functioning and resilience and negative symptoms in individuals at ultra-high risk for psychosis. Aust N Z J Psychiatry 2013;47:762-71.

226. Shin JI, Chae JH, Min JA, et al. Resilience as a possible predictor for psychological distress in chronic spinal cord injured patients living in the community. Ann Rehabil Med 2012;36:815-20.

227. Bacchi S, Licinio J. Resilience and Psychological Distress in Psychology and Medical Students. Acad Psychiatry 2016.

228. Shi M, Wang X, Bian Y, Wang L. The mediating role of resilience in the relationship between stress and life satisfaction among Chinese medical students: a cross-sectional study. BMC Med Educ 2015;15:16.

229. Dolbier CL, Jaggars SS, Steinhardt MA. Stress-related growth: pre-intervention correlates and change following a resilience intervention. Stress & Health 2010;26:135-47.

230. Li Y, Cao F, Cao D, Liu J. Nursing students' post-traumatic growth, emotional intelligence and psychological resilience. J Psychiatr Ment Health Nurs 2015;22:326-32.

231. Kemper KJ, Khirallah M. Acute Effects of Online Mind-Body Skills Training on Resilience, Mindfulness, and Empathy. J Evid Based Complementary Altern Med 2015;20:247-53.

232. Arrogante O, Perez-Garcia AM, Aparicio-Zaldivar EG. [Psychological well-being in nursing: relationships with resilience and coping]. Enferm Clin 2015;25:73-80.

233. Rahimi B, Baetz M, Bowen R, Balbuena L. Resilience, stress, and coping among Canadian medical students. Can Med Educ J 2014;5:e5-e12.

234. Campbell-Sills L, Cohan SL, Stein MB. Relationship of resilience to personality, coping, and psychiatric symptoms in young adults. Behav Res Ther 2006;44:585-99.

235. Arnetz J, Rofa Y, Arnetz B, Ventimiglia M, Jamil H. Resilience as a protective factor against the development of psychopathology among refugees. J Nerv Ment Dis 2013;201:167-72.

236. Herrmann D, Scherg H, Verres R, von Hagens C, Strowitzki T, Wischmann T. Resilience in infertile couples acts as a protective factor against infertility specific distress and impaired quality of life. J Assist Reprod Genet 2011;28:1111-7.

237. Pietrzak RH, Johnson DC, Goldstein MB, et al. Psychosocial buffers of traumatic stress, depressive symptoms, and psychosocial difficulties in veterans of Operations Enduring Freedom and Iraqi Freedom: the role of resilience, unit support, and postdeployment social support. J Spec Oper Med 2009;9:74-8.

238. Cowden RG, Meyer-Weitz A, Oppong Asante K. Mental Toughness in Competitive Tennis: Relationships with Resilience and Stress. Front Psychol 2016;7:320.

239. Secades XG, Molinero O, Salguero A, Barquin RR, de la Vega R, Marquez S. Relationship Between Resilience and Coping Strategies in Competitive Sport. Percept Mot Skills 2016;122:336-49.

240. Macedo T, Wilheim L, Goncalves R, et al. Building resilience for future adversity: a systematic review of interventions in non-clinical samples of adults. BMC Psychiatry 2014;14:227.

241. Rios-Risquez MI, Carrillo-Garcia C, Sabuco-Tebar EL, Garcia-Izquierdo M, Martinez-Roche ME. An exploratory study of the relationship between resilience, academic burnout and psychological health in nursing students. Contemp Nurse 2016:1-22.

242. Rees CS, Heritage B, Osseiran-Moisson R, et al. Can We Predict Burnout among Student Nurses? An Exploration of the ICWR-1 Model of Individual Psychological Resilience. Front Psychol 2016;7:1072.

243. Pereira JA, Barkham M, Kellett S, Saxon D. The Role of Practitioner Resilience and Mindfulness in Effective Practice: A Practice-Based Feasibility Study. Adm Policy Ment Health 2016.

244. Fred L, James BA, Bruce JA, Suzanne JP. The development and resulting performance impact of positive psychological capital. Human Resource Development Quarterly 2010;21:41-67.

245. Hartley MT. Examining the relationships between resilience, mental health, and academic persistence in undergraduate college students. J Am Coll Health 2011;59:596-604.

246. Cora-Bramble D, Zhang K, Castillo-Page L. Minority faculty members' resilience and academic productivity: are they related? Acad Med 2010;85:1492-8.

247. Robertson HD, Elliott AM, Burton C, et al. Resilience of primary healthcare professionals: a systematic review. Br J Gen Pract 2016;66:e423-33.

248. Johnson JR, Emmons HC, Rivard RL, Griffin KH, Dusek JA. Resilience Training: A Pilot Study of a Mindfulness-Based Program with Depressed Healthcare Professionals. Explore (New York, NY) 2015;11:433-44.

249. Petree RD, Broome KM, Bennett JB. Exploring and reducing stress in young restaurant workers: results of a randomized field trial. Am J Health Promot 2012;26:217-24.

250. Grant AM, Green LS, Rynsaardt J. Developmental coaching for high school teachers: Executive coaching goes to school. Consulting Psychology Journal 2010;62:151-68.

251. JM B, ML S, BL B, C H. Effects of an Online Personal Resilience Training Program for Women in Stem Doctoral Programs. . Journal of Women and Minorities in Science and Engineering 2013;19:17-35.

252. Abbott J, Klein B, Hamilton C, Rosenthal AJ. The impact of online resilience training for sales managers on wellbeing and work performance. E-Journal of Applied Psychology 2009;5:89-95.

253. Shatte A, Perlman A, Smith B, Lynch WD. The Positive Effect of Resilience on Stress and Business Outcomes in Difficult Work Environments. Journal of occupational and environmental medicine 2017;59:135-40.

254. Bengt BA, Dana CN, Mark AL, Lena B, Ake L. Trauma resilience training for police: Psychophysiological and performance effects. 2009;24:1-9.

255. Grant AM, Curtayne L, Burton G. Executive coaching enhances goal attainment, resilience and workplace well-being: A randomised controlled study. The Journal of Positive Psychology 2009;4:396-407.

256. Krage R, Zwaan L, Tjon Soei Len L, et al. Relationship between non-technical skills and technical performance during cardiopulmonary resuscitation: does stress have an influence? Emergency medicine journal : EMJ 2017;34:728-33.

257. Harker R, Pidgeon AM, Klaassen F, King S. Exploring resilience and mindfulness as preventative factors for psychological distress burnout and secondary traumatic stress among human service professionals. Work (Reading, Mass) 2016;54:631-7.

258. Ryan C, Bergin M, Chalder T, Wells JS. Web-based interventions for the management of stress in the workplace: Focus, form, and efficacy. Journal of occupational health 2017;59:215-36.

259. Eskildsen A, Andersen LP, Pedersen AD, Andersen JH. Cognitive impairments in former patients with work-related stress complaints - one year later. Stress (Amsterdam, Netherlands) 2016;19:559-66.

260. Concerto C, Patel D, Infortuna C, et al. Academic stress disrupts cortical plasticity in graduate students. Stress (Amsterdam, Netherlands) 2017;20:212-6.

261. mEquilibrium. mEquilibrium, 2018. (Accessed December 8th, 2018, 2018, at https://www.mequilibrium.com.)

262. emindful. emindful, 2018. (Accessed December 8th, 2018, 2018, at emindful.com.)

263. Benson Henry Institute. 2018. (Accessed December 8th, 2018, 2018, at https://www.bensonhenryinstitute.org.)

264. Human Performance Institute. 2018. (Accessed December 8th, 2018, 2018, at https://www.humanperformanceinstitute.com/?utm_source=google&utm_medium=cpc& utm_campaign=Brand%7CCore%20-%20BMM&utm_content=Core&utm_term=+jnj%20hpi&gclsrc=aw.ds&&gclid=EAIaIQ obChMIrcq4_6SR3wIV27rACh36yQtVEAAYASAAEgLP-_D_BwE.)

265. Astrella JA. Return on Investment: Evaluating the Evidence Regarding Financial Outcomes of Workplace Wellness Programs. The Journal of nursing administration 2017;47:379-83.

266. Baicker K, Cutler D, Song Z. Workplace wellness programs can generate savings. Health affairs (Project Hope) 2010;29:304-11.

267. Borah BJ, Egginton JS, Shah ND, et al. Association of worksite wellness center attendance with weight loss and health care cost savings: Mayo Clinic's experience. Journal of occupational and environmental medicine 2015;57:229-34.

268. Dement JM, Epling C, Joyner J, Cavanaugh K. Impacts of Workplace Health Promotion and Wellness Programs on Health Care Utilization and Costs: Results From an Academic Workplace. Journal of occupational and environmental medicine 2015;57:1159-69.

269. Schwartz SM, Mason ST, Wang C, Pomana L, Hyde-Nolan ME, Carter EW. Sustained economic value of a wellness and disease prevention program: an 8-year longitudinal evaluation. Population health management 2014;17:90-9.

270. Vaillant GE. Triumphs of Experience: The Men of the Harvard Grant Study: Belknap Press; 2012.

271. What Resilience Means, and Why It Matters. HBR, 2015. (Accessed December 8th, 2018, 2018, at https://hbr.org/2015/01/what-resilience-means-and-why-it-matters.)

272. Schaan VK, Vogele C. Resilience and rejection sensitivity mediate long-term outcomes of parental divorce. Eur Child Adolesc Psychiatry 2016.

273. Rosenberg AR, Wolfe J, Bradford MC, et al. Resilience and psychosocial outcomes in parents of children with cancer. Pediatr Blood Cancer 2014;61:552-7.

274. Pietrzak RH, Cook JM. Psychological resilience in older U.S. veterans: results from the national health and resilience in veterans study. Depress Anxiety 2013;30:432-43.

275. Waite PJ, Richardson GE. Determining the efficacy of resiliency training in the work site. J Allied Health 2004;33:178-83.

276. Herrman H, Stewart DE, Diaz-Granados N, Berger EL, Jackson B, Yuen T. What is resilience? Canadian journal of psychiatry Revue canadienne de psychiatrie 2011;56:258-65.

277. Adler AB, Williams J, McGurk D, Moss A, Bliese PD. Resilience training with soldiers during basic combat training: randomisation by platoon. Appl Psychol Health Well Being 2015;7:85-107.

278. Beck CE, Gonzales F, Jr., Sells CH, Jones C, Reer T, Zhu YY. The effects of animal-assisted therapy on wounded warriors in an Occupational Therapy Life Skills program. US Army Med Dep J 2012:38-45.

279. Cacioppo JT, Adler AB, Lester PB, et al. Building social resilience in soldiers: A double dissociative randomized controlled study. J Pers Soc Psychol 2015;109:90-105.

280. Johnson DC, Thom NJ, Stanley EA, et al. Modifying resilience mechanisms in at-risk individuals: a controlled study of mindfulness training in Marines preparing for deployment. Am J Psychiatry 2014;171:844-53.

281. Kees M, Rosenblum K. Evaluation of a psychological health and resilience intervention for military spouses: A pilot study. Psychol Serv 2015;12:222-30.

282. Kent M, Davis MC, Stark SL, Stewart LA. A resilience-oriented treatment for posttraumatic stress disorder: results of a preliminary randomized clinical trial. J Trauma Stress 2011;24:591-5.

283. Schachman KA, Lee RK, Lederma RP. Baby boot camp: facilitating maternal role adaptation among military wives. Nurs Res 2004;53:107-15.

284. Aikens KA, Astin J, Pelletier KR, et al. Mindfulness goes to work: impact of an online workplace intervention. Journal of occupational and environmental medicine 2014;56:721-31.

285. Hartfiel N, Havenhand J, Khalsa SB, Clarke G, Krayer A. The effectiveness of yoga for the improvement of well-being and resilience to stress in the workplace. Scand J Work Environ Health 2011;37:70-6.

286. Pidgeon AM, Ford L, Klaassen F. Evaluating the effectiveness of enhancing resilience in human service professionals using a retreat-based Mindfulness with Metta Training Program: a randomised control trial. Psychol Health Med 2014;19:355-64.

287. Robb SL, Burns DS, Stegenga KA, et al. Randomized clinical trial of therapeutic music video intervention for resilience outcomes in adolescents/young adults undergoing hematopoietic stem cell transplant: a report from the Children's Oncology Group. Cancer 2014;120:909-17.

288. Sharma V, Sood A, Prasad K, Loehrer L, Schroeder D, Brent B. Bibliotherapy to decrease stress and anxiety and increase resilience and mindfulness: a pilot trial. Explore (NY) 2014;10:248-52.

289. Berger R, Abu-Raiya H, Benatov J. Reducing primary and secondary traumatic stress symptoms among educators by training them to deliver a resiliency program (ERASE-Stress) following the Christchurch earthquake in New Zealand. The American journal of orthopsychiatry 2016;86:236-51.

290. Rogerson S, Meir R, Crowley-McHattan Z, McEwen K, Pastoors R. A Randomized Controlled Pilot Trial Investigating the Impact of a Workplace Resilience Program During a Time of Significant Organizational Change. Journal of occupational and environmental medicine 2016;58:329-34.

291. Erogul M, Singer G, McIntyre T, Stefanov DG. Abridged mindfulness intervention to support wellness in first-year medical students. Teach Learn Med 2014;26:350-6.

292. Fortney L, Luchterhand C, Zakletskaia L, Zgierska A, Rakel D. Abbreviated mindfulness intervention for job satisfaction, quality of life, and compassion in primary care clinicians: a pilot study. Ann Fam Med 2013;11:412-20.

293. Kanekar A, Sharma M, Atri A. Enhancing social support, hardiness, and acculturation to improve mental health among Asian Indian international students. Int Q Community Health Educ 2009;30:55-68.

294. Mache S, Vitzthum K, Klapp BF, Groneberg DA. Evaluation of a Multicomponent Psychosocial Skill Training Program for Junior Physicians in Their First Year at Work: A Pilot Study. Fam Med 2015;47:693-8.

295. Maunder RG, Lancee WJ, Mae R, et al. Computer-assisted resilience training to prepare healthcare workers for pandemic influenza: a randomized trial of the optimal dose of training. BMC Health Serv Res 2010;10:72.

296. Mealer M, Conrad D, Evans J, et al. Feasibility and acceptability of a resilience training program for intensive care unit nurses. Am J Crit Care 2014;23:e97-105.

297. Noone SJ, Hastings RP. Building psychological resilience in support staff caring for people with intellectual disabilities: pilot evaluation of an acceptance-based intervention. J Intellect Disabil 2009;13:43-53.

298. Potter P, Deshields T, Berger JA, Clarke M, Olsen S, Chen L. Evaluation of a compassion fatigue resiliency program for oncology nurses. Oncol Nurs Forum 2013;40:180-7.

299. Sood A, Prasad K, Schroeder D, Varkey P. Stress management and resilience training among Department of Medicine faculty: a pilot randomized clinical trial. J Gen Intern Med 2011;26:858-61.

300. Sood A, Sharma V, Schroeder DR, Gorman B. Stress Management and Resiliency Training (SMART) program among Department of Radiology faculty: a pilot randomized clinical trial. Explore (NY) 2014;10:358-63.

301. Steinhardt M, Dolbier C. Evaluation of a resilience intervention to enhance coping strategies and protective factors and decrease symptomatology. J Am Coll Health 2008;56:445-53.

302. Tarantino B, Earley M, Audia D, D'Adamo C, Berman B. Qualitative and quantitative evaluation of a pilot integrative coping and resiliency program for healthcare professionals. Explore (New York, NY) 2013;9:44-7.

303. Zamirinejad S, Hojjat SK, Golzari M, Borjali A, Akaberi A. Effectiveness of resilience training versus cognitive therapy on reduction of depression in female Iranian college students. Issues Ment Health Nurs 2014;35:480-8.

304. Mache S, Danzer G, Klapp B, Groneberg DA. An Evaluation of a Multicomponent Mental Competency and Stress Management Training for Entrants in Surgery Medicine. Journal of surgical education 2015;72:1102-8.

305. Bradshaw BG, Richardson GE, Kumpfer K, et al. Determining the efficacy of a resiliency training approach in adults with type 2 diabetes. Diabetes Educ 2007;33:650-9.

306. Cho EA, Oh HE. [Effects of laughter therapy on depression, quality of life, resilience and immune responses in breast cancer survivors]. J Korean Acad Nurs 2011;41:285-93.

307. Ikai S, Suzuki T, Uchida H, et al. Effects of weekly one-hour Hatha yoga therapy on resilience and stress levels in patients with schizophrenia-spectrum disorders: an eight-week randomized controlled trial. J Altern Complement Med 2014;20:823-30.

308. Kim HK, Lee M. [Effectiveness of forgiveness therapy on resilience, self-esteem, and spirituality of wives of alcoholics]. J Korean Acad Nurs 2014;44:237-47.

309. Loprinzi CE, Prasad K, Schroeder DR, Sood A. Stress Management and Resilience Training (SMART) program to decrease stress and enhance resilience among breast cancer survivors: a pilot randomized clinical trial. Clin Breast Cancer 2011;11:364-8.

310. Songprakun W, McCann TV. Evaluation of a bibliotherapy manual for reducing psychological distress in people with depression: a randomized controlled trial. J Adv Nurs 2012;68:2674-84.

311. Songprakun W, McCann TV. Effectiveness of a self-help manual on the promotion of resilience in individuals with depression in Thailand: a randomised controlled trial. BMC Psychiatry 2012;12:12.

312. Victoria Cerezo M, Ortiz-Tallo M, Cardenal V, De La Torre-Luque A. Positive psychology group intervention for breast cancer patients: a randomised trial. Psychol Rep 2014;115:44-64.

313. Wesner AC, Gomes JB, Detzel T, Guimaraes LS, Heldt E. Booster Sessions after Cognitive-Behavioural Group Therapy for Panic Disorder: Impact on Resilience, Coping, and Quality of Life. Behav Cogn Psychother 2015;43:513-25.

314. van Kessel G, MacDougall C, Gibbs L. Resilience-rhetoric to reality: a systematic review of intervention studies after disasters. Disaster Med Public Health Prep 2014;8:452-60.

Acknowledgments

I am grateful to the countless scientists, reporters, philosophers, and authors who have helped me learn the information I share in this book.

I am grateful to every person who has helped me smile, smiled at my sometimes not-so-funny jokes, and helped me keep a light heart.

I am grateful to my parents, Sahib and Shashi; my in-laws, Vinod and Kusum; my brother, Kishore; my sisters, Sandhya and Rajni; my daughters, Gauri and Sia; and my wife, Richa, for showering me with love that sustains me every day.

I am grateful to all my friends and colleagues for their support and love. I am grateful to Ann for her critical comments. I am grateful to Carla for her friendship and support. I am grateful to Debbie and Scott for their support of my work. I am grateful to Gauri for a thoughtful and comprehensive editing of the manuscript.

I am grateful to all my students and patients who trust my values and my ability to be of help. You give me strength every single day.

I am grateful to you all for helping build a kinder, happier, and more hopeful world for our planet's children. Thank you.

Amit

About Dr. Sood

Dr. Amit Sood is married to his lovely wife of 25 years, Dr. Richa Sood. They have two girls, Gauri age 14 and Sia age 8.

Dr. Sood serves as the Executive Director of Global Center for Resiliency and Wellbeing. Dr. Sood is the creator of Mayo Clinic Resilient Mind program, and is a former professor of medicine, chair of the Mind Body Medicine Initiative, and director of student life and wellness at Mayo Clinic.

Dr. Sood completed his residency in internal medicine at the Albert Einstein School of Medicine, an integrative medicine fellowship at the University of Arizona and earned a master's degree in clinical research from Mayo Clinic College of Medicine. He has received several National Institutes of Health grants and foundation awards to test and implement integrative and mind-body approaches within medicine.

Dr. Sood has developed an innovative approach toward mind-body medicine by incorporating concepts from neuroscience, evolutionary biology, psychology, philosophy and spirituality. His resulting program, Stress Management and Resiliency Training (SMART©) helps patients learn skills to decrease stress and enhance resiliency by improving self-awareness, engagement, and emotional resilience. Interventions adapted from the program reach approximately 50,000 patients and learners each year. The program has been tested in over 20 clinical trials.

Dr. Sood's programs are offered for a wide variety of patients and learners including to improve resiliency; decrease stress and anxiety; enhance well-being and happiness; cancer symptom relief and prevention; and wellness solutions for caregivers, corporate executives, health care professionals, parents, and students. SMART© program is now integrated in several hospitals and health systems for managing burnout, leadership training, for enhancing resilience among nurses, and is being offered with all ages of students, and teachers.

Dr. Sood has authored or co-authored over 70 peer-reviewed articles, and several editorials, book chapters, abstracts, and letters. He has developed award-winning patient education DVDs on topics within integrative medicine ranging from paced breathing meditation and mindfulness to wellness solutions for obesity, insomnia, and fibromyalgia. Dr. Sood is author of the books *The Mayo Clinic Guide to Stress-Free Living, The Mayo Clinic Handbook for Happiness, Immerse: A 52-Week Course in*

Resilient Living, and Mindfulness Redesigned for the Twenty-First Century. As an international expert in his field, Dr. Sood's work has been widely cited in the press including – *The Atlantic Monthly, USA Today, Wall Street Journal, New York Times, NPR, Reuters Health, Time Magazine (online), Good Housekeeping, Parenting, Real Simple, Shape, US News, Huffington Post, Mens Health Magazine, The Globe and Mail, CBS News, Fox News, and others.* He has interviewed with several prominent TV and radio shows, both nationally and internationally. He served as the February 2015 Health care pioneer for the Robert Wood Johnson Foundation.

He is a highly sought after speaker, and delivered the TEDx talk – *Happy Brain: How to Overcome Our Neural Predispositions to Suffering.* He has mentored several hundred fellows, medical students, instructors, consultants, and residents.

Dr. Sood has received several awards for his work, including the Mayo's 2010 Distinguished Service Award, Mayo's 2010 Innovator of the Year Award, Mayo's 2013 outstanding physician scientist award, and was chosen as one among the top 20 intelligent optimists "helping the world be a better place" by *Ode Magazine.*

Made in the USA
Lexington, KY
15 June 2019